The Hidden Man of the Heart

The Hidden Man of the Heart

Loving God with All Your Heart, Soul and Body

Reginald Dancil

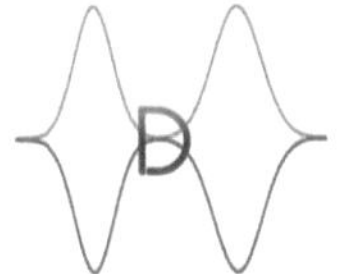

Multidimensional Management
Atlanta, GA

The Hidden Man of the Heart: Loving God with All Your Heart, Soul and Body

Learn more about the author at
www.Multidimensionalmgt.com

ISBN: 978-1-7336407-2-5 (paperback)
ISBN: 978-1-7336407-3-2 (ebook)

Library of Congress Control Number: 2026912079

Developmental editor: Annette Johnson, Allwrite Communications

Printed in the United States of America

Dedication

To my late paternal grandmother, Mrs. Almena Cooper Dancil (Mama Dancil), whose love and sacrifice shaped me into the person I am. She was a special soul.

Contents

Preface

For many years I have been fascinated by a simple question that appears often in the Scriptures: **What does it mean to believe with the heart?**

The Bible speaks frequently about the heart. We are told that with the heart man believes unto righteousness. We are warned to guard the heart, because from it flow the issues of life. We are also reminded that God looks not on the outward appearance but on the heart.

Yet despite how often the word appears in Scripture, I began to realize that many believers. including myself at times, did not fully understand what the Bible meant when it spoke about the heart.

Like many people, I had heard the word used in songs, conversations, and expressions of emotion. People spoke of loving with all their heart, having their heart broken, or following their heart. However, as I studied the Scriptures more carefully, I began to see that the biblical meaning of the heart goes far beyond emotion or sentiment.

The Bible presents the heart as the hidden center of a person's spiritual life.

It is the place where belief is formed, where trust in God is established, and where the voice of the Spirit can be heard.

As I continued studying these passages, I was drawn to a phrase written by the apostle Peter: **"the hidden man of the heart."** That expression captured my attention and began to shape my understanding of the inward life.

I began to see that the heart is not simply a poetic way of speaking about feelings. It refers to the inward spiritual person created by God—the hidden man within.

This discovery opened the door to a deeper study of how God designed human life. The Scriptures reveal that human beings are not merely physical creatures. We are **spirit, soul,** and **body**. Each part plays a role in how we live and how we relate to God.

As I studied further, the Lord began to reveal something that had not been clear to me before: the soul is not merely a collection of functions such as mind, emotion, and will. The soul is the conscious life of a person where alignment with God is either embraced or resisted. It is the "you" that loves, fears, and decides. It is the one into whom God breathed the breath of life (Genesis 2:7), and it is the one who will stand before God to give account (2 Corinthians 5:10).

When we speak to one another, we are not merely interacting with bodies. We are engaging with souls, who are living beings who perceive, respond, and choose. The eyes see, but it is the soul that perceives. The ears hear, but it is the soul that understands.

This understanding transforms how we view human life. The soul is not symbolic. It is not a representation. It is a real, living being, the person himself, temporarily clothed in a physical body but destined to live eternally.

This understanding helped me see more clearly how the spirit, soul, and body work together in the life of a believer.

- The spirit, the hidden man of the heart, communicates with God.
- The soul processes thoughts, emotions, and decisions.
- The body expresses outwardly what the spirit and soul have agreed upon.

When these three parts function in harmony, life begins to reflect the order God intended. However, when they fall out of alignment, confusion often follows. The mind may struggle with doubt. Emotions may react with fear. The will may hesitate to follow the direction that the spirit has received from God.

Learning how these dimensions of life work together has helped me understand many of the spiritual struggles believers face. More importantly, it has helped me see how God brings restoration and alignment to the inner life.

This book grew out of that journey of discovery. It is not merely the result of academic study but also the fruit of personal experiences in which the Lord has taught me about fear, faith, obedience, and the inward life of the believer.

My hope is that the ideas presented in these pages will help readers better understand how God designed them to live. When we recognize the role of the heart, understand the function of the soul, and learn to present our bodies in obedience to God, we begin to experience life as God intended—from the inside out.

It is my prayer that this book will encourage you to listen more carefully to the voice of God within the hidden man of the heart and to allow His Spirit to bring your spirit, soul, and body into harmony with His purposes.

~ *Reginald Carl Dancil*

Acknowledgements

Thank you to my best friend Joyce Smith; god-daughter and heart string Stephanie Rogers; godsons Brandon Smith and Brian Johnson; god-children Carman Johnson Small and Ashley Dixon Lloyd; mentor Bishop Kirby Clements Sr; and my Lord and Savior Jesus.

To friends and family not mentioned, you know I love and respect your input into my life.

Special thanks to Ms. Annette R. Johnson for her sensitivity in understanding the purpose and direction of my thoughts. It is as if she and I were of the same mind and spirit.

Introduction

The Question Behind the Word "Heart"

We use the word *heart* thousands of times without thinking. We say, "I love you with all my heart." We speak of heartbreak, cold-heartedness, and tender hearts. We promise from the heart and forgive from the heart. Yet when Scripture commands us to believe with the heart, guard the heart, or love God with all the heart, few can clearly define what that heart actually is.

The Bible does not use words carelessly. When Jesus said, "With the heart man believeth unto righteousness," He was not referring to emotion. When Scripture warns that the heart can be deceitful, it is not speaking of a physical organ. The heart described in Scripture is neither sentiment nor muscle. It is the spiritual core of the human being.

Humanity is tri-part in design. Man is a spirit. He has a soul. He lives in a body. Confusion about the heart often arises because these three dimensions are blended together in everyday language. Emotion is mistaken for spirit. Thought is mistaken for conscience. The inward man is reduced to feeling. However, Scripture distinguishes carefully. The Word of God is said to divide between soul and spirit. This means there is a difference. And if there is a difference, it must matter.

This book is a structured exploration of that distinction. It seeks to answer foundational questions:

What does it mean to believe with the heart?
What is the hidden man of the heart?
How does the spirit relate to the soul?
Why must the heart be guarded?
What evidence reveals whether the inward man is aligned with God?

These are not abstract theological questions. They determine how one lives, how one responds under pressure, how one hears the voice of God, and how one walks in faith rather than fear.

The hidden man of the heart is not poetic language. He is the inward spiritual being created to commune with God. When regenerated, he is clothed in meekness and quiet confidence. When neglected, the soul dominates and confusion follows.

The world teaches that life flows from the outside in — from circumstances, influence, and environment. Scripture teaches the opposite. "Out of the heart are the issues of life." Life flows from within.

To understand the heart is to understand the seat of belief. To understand the inward man is to understand spiritual authority. To guard the heart is to protect the source of thought, speech, and action.

This book is written not merely to inform but to clarify, separating what has been blended and restoring what has been misunderstood. It is a call to live from the spirit rather than from the turbulence of the soul. For when the hidden man of the heart is rightly understood, the believer learns to believe from the place God designed and to live from the inside out.

Ultimately, this book is an exploration of what it means to love God with the whole person. When Jesus taught that the greatest commandment is to love God with all our heart, soul, mind, and strength (Matthew 22:37, Mark 12:30, Luke 10:27), He was describing the totality of human life. This is not merely a call to emotion or devotion, but an invitation for every part of our inner and outer life to be brought into harmony with God. In this book, that outward expression of strength is understood through the body, the means by which love for God is lived and made visible. In its fullness, this means:

- To love God with the heart is to believe Him.
- To love God with the soul is to bring our thoughts, emotions, and will into alignment with His truth.
- To love God with the body is to express that love through obedience and daily living.

What follows is a journey into that reality, from the hidden man of the heart to the outward life that flows from it.

PART I – THE HEART

The Hidden Man and the Place of Belief

Chapter 1

The Language of the Heart

The word *heart* is one of the most commonly used words in human language. We use it in everyday conversation, in songs, in poetry, and in expressions of love, grief, loyalty, and devotion. Yet despite how frequently we speak of the heart, few people can clearly explain what the heart truly is. This raises an important question that often goes unexamined: What do we actually mean when we use the word "**heart**"?

People say things like:

"I love you with all my heart."

"My heart belongs to you."

"She broke my heart."

"He has a heart of gold."

"God knows my heart."

"Follow your heart."

In moments of sincerity, people often place their hand over their chest as they speak these words, instinctively pointing to the physical location of the organ that pumps blood through the body. In ordinary conversation this gesture feels natural. However, when we pause and examine what we are actually saying, a subtle tension begins to emerge. Something about it does not fully make sense.

When a person says, "I give you my heart," they obviously do not mean the physical organ inside their chest. If they did, they would not survive the gift. Likewise, when someone says their heart has been broken, they are not describing a medical condition involving the failure of the heart muscle. Something deeper is being expressed.

Taken together, these expressions reveal something significant: The language of the heart is emotional, relational, and deeply human. It communicates attachment, trust, loyalty, pain, and devotion. In many ways it is the language people use when they want to express the deepest part of themselves.

This language appears not only in conversation but also in music and poetry. Songs have long captured the emotional weight people attach to the heart. Lyrics speak of leaving one's heart in a city, of listening to one's heart, of following the heart wherever it leads. Other songs speak of broken hearts, lonely hearts, foolish hearts, and hardened hearts.

All of these expressions assume that the heart represents something more than flesh and blood. They point to a deeper reality that cannot be seen but is clearly experienced. They suggest that the heart is somehow connected to the inner life of a person, the place where love, sorrow, hope, and belief reside.

This understanding is not limited to human expression. Scripture uses the same language. The Bible speaks of a "broken heart," a "pure heart," a "deceitful heart," and a "new heart." God promises through the prophet Ezekiel that He will remove a heart of stone and replace it with a heart of flesh (36:26). These descriptions clearly do not refer to a physical transplant of the organ within the chest. They refer to something deeper within the inner life of the human being.

With all of this in view, the question then becomes unavoidable:

What *is* the heart?

Most people cannot answer that question with clarity. When asked directly, they often hesitate. Some will simply point to their chest. Others will say the heart represents emotions or feelings. Still others may say it refers to love. However, the Scriptures suggest something far more profound.

Before turning to the Bible's explanation, it is important to see how this question moves beyond theory and into real human experience. I remember a moment from my childhood when the meaning of a broken heart became painfully real to me.

I was born out of wedlock and during my early years lived with my mother and her husband. Those early years were difficult and marked by physical abuse. My mother eventually became concerned for my safety and contacted my father and his mother about the possibility of caring for me. At the time, I was probably 5 or 6 years old.

My mother, my father, and my paternal grandmother met to discuss my future. The decision was made that my grandmother, "Mama Dancil," would take me into her home for what I was told would be a short stay while my parents went to a movie. What I did not understand at the time was that this "short stay" would last the rest of my childhood.

After dinner that evening, my grandmother told me it was time to take a bath and get ready for bed. I remember being confused. I thought, *Bed? Why was I going to bed there?*

Suddenly the realization hit me with overwhelming force: my mother was not coming back that night. In fact, she would not be coming back at all. In that moment my heart was broken. I felt abandoned, deserted, and alone. I remember lying in bed and looking back toward the doorway, hoping my mother would return. The next thing I remember was waking the next morning still hoping she might come.

Mama Dancil turned out to be a blessing in my life, a true gift from God. She loved and cared for me faithfully. Yet even with that love and care, no one could fill the place that belonged to my mother.

That early experience revealed something I could not have understood otherwise about the language of the heart. When people say their heart is broken, they are describing a wound that cannot be measured by doctors or repaired with medicine. It is a wound that exists somewhere deep inside the person. It affects thoughts, emotions, relationships, and even the way a person sees the world. Only God can truly heal that kind of brokenness.

Over the years, that experience led me to ask deeper questions. I have spoken with many people about the heart and have often asked them what they believe the heart actually is. Most admit they have never seriously thought about the question. Yet the Bible places enormous importance on the heart. Scripture teaches that a person believes with the heart. It teaches that the heart can rejoice or be troubled. It warns that the heart can be deceived. It commands us to guard the heart carefully because the issues of life flow from it.

If the heart plays such a central role in spiritual life, then understanding what the heart truly is becomes essential. It cannot simply be the physical organ in our chest. The heart described in Scripture must be something deeper, something capable of believing, trusting, fearing, rejoicing, and communicating with God.

The Bible presents the heart as the spiritual center of the human being. It is the place where belief takes root, where devotion forms, and where the deepest decisions of life are made. Understanding this becomes essential. In the chapters that follow, we will examine what Scripture reveals about this mysterious inner reality. We will explore the relationship between the heart, the soul, and the body, and we will seek to understand the hidden dimension of human life that God created for communion with Himself.

For when we truly understand what the Bible means by the heart, we begin to understand who we are and how God intended us to live from the inside out.

Chapter 2

What the Bible Means by Heart

If the word *heart* is used so often in both everyday language and Scripture, then it becomes essential to understand what the Bible actually means when it uses the term. As we saw in the previous chapter, people commonly associate the heart with emotions or feelings. While emotions may be expressed through the heart, the biblical meaning goes far deeper.

The Scriptures describe the heart as the inner center of the human being—the place where belief, devotion, and moral direction originate. The heart is not the physical organ within the chest. Instead, it refers to the spiritual core of a person.

The apostle Paul makes this clear when he writes about salvation:

> *"That if thou shalt confess with thy mouth the Lord Jesus, and shalt believe in thine heart that God hath raised him from the dead, thou shalt be saved. For with the heart man believeth unto righteousness; and with the mouth confession is made unto salvation."* (Romans 10:9–10)

This passage reveals something important. Belief, the kind that leads to righteousness, does not originate merely in intellectual agreement.

It occurs in the heart. The mouth may confess, but the confession only carries power when it expresses what has already been believed in the heart. In other words, the heart is the place where faith takes root. This establishes the heart not as a passive container of feeling, but as an active center of belief.

Jesus also spoke of the heart as the place where doubt and belief reside. When teaching about faith, He said:

> *"Have faith in God... Truly I tell you, if anyone says to this mountain, 'Go, throw yourself into the sea,' and does not doubt in their heart but believes what they say will happen, it will be done for them." (Mark 11:22–23)*

Here again the heart appears as the center of belief. Faith and doubt are not merely intellectual concepts; they arise from the inner life of the person.

Beyond belief, the heart also reveals what a person values most. Jesus explained this when He said:

> *"For where your treasure is, there your heart will be also."* (Matthew 6:21)

This statement reveals that the heart is the place where priorities are established. What a person truly values – whether material possessions, personal ambition, or devotion to God – reveals where their heart resides.

In addition to belief and values, Scripture also shows that the heart experiences emotional responses such as joy, fear, and trouble. When speaking to His disciples before His crucifixion, Jesus said:

> *"Do not let your hearts be troubled. You believe in God; believe also in me."* (John 14:1)

Here the heart is portrayed as the place where anxiety and peace are experienced. It is the inner center where confidence or fear can develop depending on where trust is placed. Because of this central role, Scripture repeatedly warns believers to guard it carefully. The book of Proverbs gives this instruction:

> *"Above all else, guard your heart, for everything you do flows from it."* (Proverbs 4:23)

This verse reveals that the heart is the source from which life's actions and attitudes flow. Words, decisions, relationships, and behavior all originate in the heart. For this reason, protecting the heart from corruption and deception is essential.

Yet the Bible also presents a sobering truth about the human heart. Left to itself, the heart can become deeply corrupted. The prophet Jeremiah describes the natural condition of the human heart with striking honesty:

> *"The heart is deceitful above all things and beyond cure. Who can understand it?"* (Jeremiah 17:9)

This verse does not mean that every human intention is evil, but it does remind us that the heart is capable of self-deception. People can justify actions, rationalize wrong choices, and persuade themselves that destructive paths are acceptable. Because of this tendency, the heart requires divine transformation.

God promises such transformation in the book of Ezekiel:

> *"I will give them an undivided heart and put a new spirit in them; I will remove from them their heart of stone and give them a heart of flesh."* (11:19)

The image of a "heart of stone" represents spiritual hardness, an inner condition that resists God's direction. A "heart of flesh," on the other hand, represents a responsive heart, softened and renewed by God's Spirit. This promise reveals that the ultimate solution to the problem of the human heart is not self-improvement but spiritual renewal. God Himself must change the heart.

A Hardened Heart

To see how this plays out in real life, Scripture provides a distinct example. One of the clearest biblical examples of the heart is found in the life of Pharaoh during the Exodus. Pharaoh was not ignorant of what God was saying. Through Moses and Aaron, he heard the command of the Lord clearly: "Let my people go" (Exodus 5:1–2). He also witnessed signs and wonders that confirmed the authority behind that command.

Yet Pharaoh's response reveals something important about the heart. His resistance was not due to a lack of information, but a refusal to yield. So, the issue was not clarity, but surrender. His position, pride, and sense of authority caused him to reject what he knew to be true. He asked, "Who is the Lord, that I should obey him?" (Exodus 5:2), revealing that the issue was not understanding, but submission.

Scripture repeatedly describes Pharaoh's heart as hardened (Exodus 7:13). This hardening did not occur in a single moment but developed through repeated resistance to the word of God. Each time truth was presented, Pharaoh chose to resist it, and that resistance strengthened the condition of his heart.

This example helps clarify what the Bible means by the heart. The heart is not merely emotional. It is the place of decision, where a person either yields to God or resists Him. When the heart consistently rejects truth, it becomes hardened—insensitive, resistant, and unwilling to respond.

The account of Pharaoh also reveals an important principle. God does not force obedience upon the heart. Rather, He allows the heart to follow the direction it has chosen. What begins as resistance can become a fixed condition if it is continually reinforced.

In this way, the heart determines the course of a person's life. It can remain open to God, or it can become hardened through pride and repeated disobedience.

A Pure Heart

If Pharaoh reveals the danger of a hardened heart, Scripture also presents the ideal: a heart that is open, responsive, and aligned with God. Jesus spoke of this condition in the Sermon on the Mount, saying, "Blessed are the pure in heart, for they shall see God" (Matthew 5:8). A pure heart is not defined by outward perfection, but by inward alignment. It is a heart that is submitted to God, committed to His ways, and responsive to His presence.

This truth is reinforced in the Old Testament when the Lord spoke to Samuel as he considered the outward appearance of Eliab, Jesse's oldest son. God said, "People look at the outward appearance, but the Lord looks at the heart" (1 Samuel 16:7). This reveals that the heart, not external behavior alone, is the primary focus of God's evaluation.

A pure heart is shaped by what it receives and regards. Scripture says, "I have hidden your word in my heart that I might not sin against you" (Psalm 119:11). The Word of God, planted within the heart, acts as a stabilizing, sanctifying force. It does not eliminate the possibility of sin, but it interrupts its dominance and redirects the life. It becomes a point of conviction, guidance, and correction.

The apostle John writes that those who are born of God do not continue in sin as a way of life, because God's seed remains in them (1 John 3:9). This speaks to a transformed nature. The inward man is no longer governed by sin, but by the life of God within.

A pure heart, therefore, is not sinless in performance, but transformed in nature. It is a heart that has been awakened to God, shaped by His Word, and guided by His Spirit. It is sensitive, responsive, and aligned. Such a heart does not merely know about God, it perceives Him. It recognizes His presence, responds to His voice, and lives in fellowship with Him.

A Heart That Seeks God

Scripture provides a powerful example of what it means to live from the heart. David is described as "a man after God's own heart" (1 Samuel 13:14; Acts 13:22). This description does not suggest that David was without fault. In fact, his life includes moments of significant failure. Yet despite those failures, something remained true about the posture of his heart. His life demonstrates that the defining quality of the heart is not perfection, but direction.

David's relationship with God was rooted in sincerity, responsiveness, and continual return. When he sinned, he did not harden his heart but turned back to God in repentance. In Psalm 51, he prayed, "Create in me a clean heart, O God, and renew a right spirit within me" (Psalm 51:10). This prayer reveals an awareness that the condition of the heart determines the condition of the life.

God's evaluation of David reminds us that He does not measure a person in the same way that people do. When Samuel the prophet saw David as only a shepherd of livestock, God saw a shepherd of His people. To be a person after God's heart is not to be perfect, but to be aligned, continually returning, responding, and remaining open to Him. The hidden man of the heart is, therefore, the true center of spiritual life.

Who Knows the Heart

Finally, the Scriptures also reveal that God actively examines the heart. Jeremiah continues:

> *"I the Lord search the heart and examine the mind, to reward each person according to their conduct."* (Jeremiah 17:10)

Unlike human observers who can only see outward behavior, God looks directly into the heart. He sees motives, intentions, and desires that may remain hidden from everyone else. This is why the Bible repeatedly calls people to sincerity before God. The condition of the heart matters more than outward appearances.

Taken together, the passages in this chapter reveal several important characteristics of the heart. According to Scripture, the heart is the place where:

- faith or doubt develops
- values and priorities are formed
- emotions such as fear or joy arise
- moral decisions are made
- devotion to God is expressed

The heart believes, hopes, fears, rejoices, and chooses. It is the deepest part of human identity. However, the Bible goes even further. Scripture does not simply describe the heart as a metaphor for inner feelings. It speaks of the heart as a real, living dimension of the human being, a hidden inner person who exists beyond what the eyes can see. The apostle Peter describes this inner reality when he writes:

> *"Rather, it should be that of your inner self, the unfading beauty of a gentle and quiet spirit, which is of great worth in God's sight."* (1 Peter 3:4)

Peter refers to this inner self as the hidden man of the heart. This statement raises a remarkable possibility: the heart may not merely be an emotional center but the dwelling place of an inward spiritual person. This means the heart is not just something that feels, but rather, it is someone who reflects who we *truly* are. If this is true, then understanding the heart requires us to explore a deeper question: **Who is the hidden man of the heart?**

The next chapter will examine this mysterious inner reality and explain how the hidden man relates to the spirit of man and to God Himself.

Chapter 3

The Spirit, Soul, and Body of Man

Before we can fully understand the hidden man of the heart, we must first understand how the Bible describes the structure of human life. **Without this foundation, the concept of the heart remains incomplete.** Scripture teaches that human beings are not composed of only a physical body. Instead, the Bible presents humanity as a three-part being.

The apostle Paul writes:

> *"And the very God of peace sanctify you wholly; and I pray God your whole spirit and soul and body be preserved blameless unto the coming of our Lord Jesus Christ."* (1 Thessalonians 5:23)

This verse identifies the three dimensions of human life: spirit, soul, and body. These are not interchangeable terms, but distinct dimensions that work together to form a unified life.

The body is the physical dimension of life. Through the body we interact with the material world. Our senses allow us to see, hear, touch, taste, and smell. The body enables us to move through the world and express ourselves through action.

This body was not accidental or incomplete. It was intricately designed with systems necessary for life, including the skeletal, muscular, nervous, cardiovascular, digestive, and respiratory systems. Each works together in remarkable order. Yet for all its complexity, the body was never intended to function as the source of life itself. It was the vessel.

Life began when God breathed into man. At that moment, man did not simply become alive in a physical sense. He became a conscious being capable of thought, emotion, and choice. He could think, feel, and respond. He could know and relate to God.

This moment reveals something essential about human identity. The body provides structure, but the soul represents the conscious life within that structure, the dimension through which a person thinks, feels, and chooses. The breath of God did not merely activate biological function; it brought forth a being who could know God, respond to Him, and live in relationship with Him.

This distinction becomes clearer when we return to the origin of human life. The book of Genesis tells us that God formed the body of man from the dust of the earth. Then God breathed into him the breath of life, and the man became a "living soul" (Genesis 2:7). In that moment, the spirit of life given by God entered the human body, and the person became a living being.

Yet even beyond body and soul lies another dimension of human life: **the spirit**. The spirit is the deepest part of human nature. It is the part of a person created to commune with God. While the body connects us with the physical world and the soul connects us with our own thoughts and emotions, the spirit connects us with the Creator. Together, these three dimensions form the complete structure of human life.

This structure explains much about human experience:

- The body interacts with the world.
- The soul processes experience.
- The spirit connects with God.

Understanding these distinctions is essential because the Bible also teaches that the spirit and the soul are not the same thing.

When God formed man from the dust of the ground, which is the body, and breathed into him the breath of life, Scripture does not say that man became a living body or even a living spirit. It says that man became a living soul. This statement is foundational. It reveals that the identity of the human being is not rooted merely in physical form or even in spiritual capacity alone, but is expressed through the living soul, where a person becomes aware of thought, emotion, and choice. The soul is the dimension through which that inner life is experienced and expressed, but it is not the deepest source of life itself.

Understanding the Structure of Human Life

To make this clearer, we can revisit each dimension with greater precision. The Word of God is described as capable of "dividing between soul and spirit" (Hebrews 4:12). If they can be divided, then they must be distinct. This distinction becomes extremely important when we begin to examine the heart.

The heart, as described in Scripture, is not merely the seat of emotion. It is the inward spiritual person, the hidden man through whom God communicates with human beings. To understand the heart properly, we must first recognize the role of the spirit within the structure of human life. Only then can we begin to understand what Scripture means when it speaks of believing with the heart.

To understand the hidden man of the heart, it helps to picture how the different parts of human life relate to one another. Scripture describes human beings as spirit, soul, and body. These are not separate persons living inside the same individual, but three dimensions of one unified life working together.

The body is the outward and visible dimension of human existence. Through the body we interact with the physical world using our senses of sight, hearing, touch, taste, and smell. The body allows us to move, speak, work, and relate to others within the material world. It is the instrument through which the inner life expresses itself outwardly.

The soul represents the inner life of thought and emotion. Within the soul a person becomes aware of themselves and their surroundings. The mind reasons and reflects on experience. The emotions respond to events with joy, sorrow, fear, or hope. The will chooses how a person will respond to the situations they face. Through these faculties the soul interprets life and makes decisions.

The spirit, however, occupies a deeper dimension of human existence. The spirit is the part of a person created to commune with God. While the body connects us with the physical world and the soul allows us to experience and interpret life, the spirit allows us to know God. It is through the spirit that faith arises, that the voice of the Holy Spirit is recognized, and that a person becomes aware of spiritual truth. Basically, it is the dimension of life where trust develops, where truth is recognized, and where communion with God becomes real.

Because these dimensions interact continuously, it may be helpful to think of them in terms of direction. The spirit is God-conscious, the soul is self-conscious, and the body is world-conscious. Understanding this distinction is essential, because confusion between these dimensions leads to confusion in spiritual life.

Each dimension contributes something important to the experience of life, yet Scripture suggests that human life functions best when these parts operate in the order God intended. When the spirit, made alive to God through Jesus Christ, receives guidance by the Holy Spirit, the soul interprets and applies that guidance through thought, emotion, and decision. The body then expresses those decisions through actions in the world. In this way, the inner life shapes the outward life.

However, when this order becomes reversed and the soul attempts to lead without guidance from the spirit, confusion often results. Thoughts become dominated by human reasoning alone, emotions react strongly to circumstances, and decisions may be guided more by impulse than by spiritual wisdom. The struggle many believers experience in their spiritual lives often occurs within this tension between the spirit and the soul.

For this reason, the Word of God is described as capable of dividing between soul and spirit. Scripture reveals the difference between what originates from the spirit and what arises from the soul. As the believer learns to recognize that distinction, the inner life gradually comes into alignment with God's design.

Understanding this structure prepares us to explore the next question in greater depth: If the spirit is the place where God communicates with humanity, who is the hidden man of the heart described by Peter?

The Fracture of Communion

In the beginning, humanity was created to live in direct and unhindered communion with God. There was no separation, no confusion, and no resistance within the inner life. Man's spirit was alive to God, responsive to His voice, and fully aligned with His presence. There was no separation, no confusion, and no resistance within the inner life.

This communion was spirit to Spirit. God, who is Spirit, communicated directly with the spirit of man, establishing a relationship that was immediate and unbroken. The soul and body functioned in harmony under this divine order. Thought, emotion, and will were not independent forces but expressions flowing from a spirit that was fully yielded to God. In this state, man did not struggle to discern God's voice. He lived in it.

That order, however, was disrupted when sin entered through disobedience. Genesis records that after eating from the tree, Adam and Eve hid themselves from the presence of the Lord among the trees of the garden (Genesis 3:8). This was the first indication that something within had shifted. The openness that once defined their relationship with God was replaced by fear and withdrawal. What had been natural now became strained.

The consequences of this act extended beyond a single moment. God placed cherubim and a flaming sword to guard the way to the Tree of Life (Genesis 3:24). While no veil existed in Eden as it later would in the Temple, this act functioned in the same way. It revealed that access to God's presence was now restricted. His holiness could no longer be approached in the same manner, and humanity could no longer live in the fullness of immediate communion as before.

With this separation came an internal reordering. The spirit of man, once the primary point of connection with God, no longer governed as it had in the beginning. The soul moved into a place of prominence. What was designed to follow began to lead. Human life became increasingly directed by thought, emotion, and personal will rather than by the direct leading of God. What man could reason, feel, and perceive began to shape his decisions more than what God revealed.

This shift explains the condition of human experience. The soul, though essential, was never designed to lead. It was created to respond to the spirit, not replace it. When the soul assumes control, life becomes centered on self rather than on God. Reasoning attempts to replace revelation. Emotion begins to dictate truth. The will seeks independence rather than surrender. The result is an inner life that is active, yet often misaligned.

The story of Scripture reveals that this separation was never intended to be permanent. What was introduced in the garden finds its answer in the work of Jesus Christ. When He was crucified, the veil of the Temple was torn from top to bottom (Matthew 27:51), signifying that the barrier between God and man had been removed.

This restored access, however, is not independent of Christ. Scripture declares that there is "one mediator between God and mankind, the man Christ Jesus" (1 Timothy 2:5). Jesus, as our High Priest, has made a way for humanity to come into the presence of God. Through Him, what was once restricted is now opened. So, what was lost in the garden was restored through the cross.

Because of this, the believer is invited to come boldly before God, not in personal merit, but through the finished work of Christ (Hebrews 4:14–16). Communion with God has been restored, yet it is always rooted in relationship with Jesus. There is no return to God apart from Him, but in Him there is full and unhindered access.

Through Christ, the spirit of man is made alive again to God. Communion is restored, not as a distant concept, but as a present reality. Yet the effects of the original disruption remain within the soul. The mind still reasons independently. The emotions still fluctuate. The will still resists surrender. This is why spiritual growth involves more than receiving new life. It requires the restoration of proper order within the inner man.

Understanding this fracture is essential. It explains why the soul often struggles, why the mind becomes a battleground, and why the believer must learn to live from the spirit rather than from the impulses of the soul. What was lost in the garden has been restored in Christ, but it must now be lived out through alignment, renewal, and submission to God.

Simple Picture of the Inner Life

At this point, it may be helpful to summarize the relationship between spirit, soul, and body in a simple way. What has been explained in detail can now be seen as a unified pattern.

Human life functions much like a series of connected layers in which the inner dimension influences what follows outwardly. When the order operates as God intended, the spirit receives direction from God, the soul interprets that direction through thought and decision, and the body expresses those decisions through action in the world.

The spirit may therefore be understood as the place of communion with God. It is the dimension of life in which faith arises and where the voice of the Holy Spirit is recognized. The soul serves as the interpreter of that inward guidance. Through the mind, emotions, and will, the soul processes what the spirit receives and determines how a person will respond. The body then becomes the instrument through which those responses appear in visible form.

When this order remains intact, the inward life gradually shapes the outward life. Thoughts become aligned with truth, emotions begin to follow faith rather than fear, and actions reflect the character formed within. Spiritual maturity often involves learning to allow the spirit to guide the soul rather than allowing the soul to react first and attempt to guide the spirit.

This pattern will become increasingly important as the discussion continues. The chapters that follow will explore the hidden man of the heart and the role the spirit plays in receiving direction from God. Once that foundation is clear, we will then examine how the soul learns to follow that guidance and how the body ultimately expresses the life that begins within. This distinction is essential, because to love God with all the heart, soul, and body is not simply a command to feel more deeply, but a call to engage every dimension of life in right relationship with Him.

Chapter 4

The Hidden Man of the Heart

If the Bible speaks of the heart as the center of belief, devotion, and moral decision, then an important question follows: **Who or what is the heart?** The Scriptures give a remarkable answer. The apostle Peter writes:

> *"Rather, it should be that of your inner self, the unfading beauty of a gentle and quiet spirit, which is of great worth in God's sight."* (1 Peter 3:4)

In this passage, Peter refers to **"the hidden man of the heart."** This phrase suggests that within every human being there exists an inner spiritual person, an unseen dimension of life that cannot be observed with physical eyes. This is not a metaphor, but a reality that reshapes how we understand the heart entirely. Chapter 3 revealed the structure of human life. This chapter reveals the spiritual person within it.

To understand the hidden man of the heart is to understand where love for God truly begins. Jesus did not call us to love God superficially, but from the deepest place within us. To love God with the heart is to trust Him, believing His Word and voice above what is seen, felt, or reasoned. It is within the heart that faith is fostered, and without faith, it is impossible to please God (Hebrews 11:6). This means that love for God is not proven externally first, but internally established. The condition of the heart, therefore, determines the authenticity of love. A heart aligned with

God becomes the source from which all true devotion flows.

David was fully committed to achieving this, praying in Psalm 86: 11-12 for guidance, an undivided heart, and the ability to walk in truth, followed by a vow to praise God wholeheartedly. He was asking for a heart that is not torn between competing loyalties, such as materialism or pride, but focused entirely on God. He wanted to love and praise God sincerely with all his heart, and he asked God to "teach" him.

Identity of the Inward Man

Like David, we should not only seek clear direction, but we should also desire a sincere understanding. At this point, it becomes important to define more precisely what is meant by the heart, the hidden man, and the spirit. These terms are closely related, but they are not identical, and clarity here will shape everything that follows.

The heart can be understood as the inward center of human life, the unseen place where belief, desire, and response to God occur. Within that center is the hidden man of the heart, the inward spiritual person who lives beneath outward behavior and natural awareness. The human spirit is the deepest dimension of that inward person. It is the part of the hidden man through which communion with God takes place.

In simple terms, the heart is the place, the hidden man is the person within that place, and the spirit is the part of that person that knows God. This distinction is essential. When Scripture speaks of the heart, it is not referring merely to emotion, but to the inward life where the hidden man resides. When it speaks of the spirit, it points to the deepest level of that inward life where God is known and received.

This distinction between the outward person and the inward person appears throughout Scripture. While the outward man is visible, the hidden man lives within. Human beings often focus on external appearance, such as what can be seen, measured, and evaluated by the senses. God, however, consistently directs attention to the inner life.

The hidden man of the heart is the spiritual being within the human person. It is the dimension of life created to communicate with God. While the body interacts with the physical world through the senses and the soul processes thoughts and emotions, the hidden man of the heart connects with the Creator.

This inner person is not imaginary or symbolic. According to Scripture, it is the true spiritual core of a human being. When a person becomes aware of this inward reality, they begin to understand that human life is more than physical existence or intellectual activity. There is a deeper dimension of life where God communicates, guides, and transforms. The hidden man of the heart is the place where that interaction occurs.

Dress of the Inward Man

If the heart is a person, then that person has a nature. Scripture even describes how this inward man is "clothed." The outward man is dressed with clothing, ornaments, and other physical expressions. The hidden man, however, is adorned in a different way. Peter says that the inward person is clothed with **a meek and quiet spirit**, a quality that is of great value in the sight of God (1 Peter 3:4).

Although Peter speaks in this passage within the context of

instruction to women, the qualities he describes are not limited to one group. The meek and quiet spirit is not a gender-specific attribute but a description of the nature of the inward man as it relates to God. These qualities define how the spirit of man responds to the Spirit of God – with humility, receptivity, and trust.

Meekness is often misunderstood. In the world's thinking, meekness is associated with weakness or passivity. Scripture, however, presents meekness in a very different light. Meekness is strength under control. It is the willingness to surrender one's own agenda and submit to the wisdom and direction of God. A meek spirit recognizes that God possesses infinite knowledge and perfect understanding and, therefore, chooses to trust His guidance. Rather than insisting on personal control, the meek heart yields itself to divine direction.

This does not mean the meek person lacks conviction or courage. On the contrary, true meekness is often displayed most clearly in moments of pressure and adversity. Jesus Himself demonstrated this strength when He faced the cross. Despite suffering injustice and cruelty, He prayed, "Father, forgive them, for they do not know what they are doing." His response revealed a spirit that was fully aligned with the will of God rather than driven by anger or revenge. In this way, meekness becomes the posture that allows the inward man to remain aligned with God.

The same quality can be seen in the apostles who continued to proclaim the message of Christ even when threatened by authorities. Their confidence did not come from personal power but from their relationship with God. This is the nature of a meek spirit: firm, disciplined, and guided by divine purpose.

Alongside meekness, Peter describes the hidden man as possessing a **quiet spirit**. Quietness in this context does not refer to silence or timidity. Instead, it describes a spirit that listens before speaking and receives instruction before acting.

A quiet spirit is attentive to the voice of God. It is not passive, but responsive. Rather than rushing to express personal opinions or strategies, the quiet heart waits for divine direction. It seeks understanding from the Holy Spirit and speaks only as it is led. In this way the hidden man becomes the place where communication with God occurs.

The Voice of the Spirit

The Scriptures repeatedly describe this relationship between the spirit of man and the Spirit of God. What has been described conceptually now becomes relational. God speaks, and the hidden man hears. The inward person receives instruction, guidance, correction, and encouragement from the Holy Spirit. Jesus described this relationship when He said: *"My sheep hear my voice, and I know them, and they follow me"* (John 10:27). Hearing, in this sense, is relational first.

Hearing the voice of God is not merely a physical experience through the ears. It is primarily a spiritual experience within the heart. The hidden man of the heart recognizes the voice of the Shepherd and responds in obedience. Because of this relationship, the hidden man becomes the center of spiritual life. Faith, trust, and obedience all originate from this inner place.

Essentially, the hidden man of the heart is the place where God communicates with man. This communication does not originate in the natural mind, but in the spirit. The Spirit of God speaks to the spirit of man, and from that place, understanding begins to unfold. Scripture refers to this as "prophecy," which in its simplest form is the speaking forth of the mind and counsel of God. While many associate prophecy with predicting future events, its primary function is to declare what God is saying in the present for the purpose of strengthening, encouraging, and directing His people (1 Corinthians 14:3).

This communication is not dependent on human ability. It flows from the relationship between the Spirit of God and the inward man. The soul may interpret it and the body may express it, but its origin is always spiritual. Thus, the believer must learn to recognize the voice of God within. The hidden man of the heart is designed to hear Him.

When the heart is aligned with God, the entire person begins to move in harmony with His will. The hidden man also serves as the place where divine guidance flows into the rest of the human personality. What is received in the spirit influences the thoughts of the soul and ultimately directs the actions of the body. In this way, the inner life shapes the outward life.

When fellowship with God is strong, the heart becomes a source of peace and clarity. When that fellowship is neglected or broken, the heart may become troubled, fearful, or confused. This is why the condition of the heart is so important.

The hidden man of the heart was created to live in communion with God. When that relationship is restored through faith, the inward person begins to experience transformation. The qualities described by Peter – meekness, quietness, reverence, and submission – become the natural character of the heart. These qualities are not produced by human effort alone. They grow out of a living relationship with God.

The hidden man of the heart is not only the place of belief, but also the place of communication. It is here that God speaks, not through natural reasoning, but through the spirit.

Learning to Follow the Voice Within

This inward communication is not theoretical. It operates in real, everyday decisions. In early 2025, I began looking for a storage rack for my extensive collection of CDs I had amassed over the years. I searched online and in stores but could not find what I wanted. One day, while resting, I began to see in my mind a different kind of rack, not vertical, but horizontal. The impression was clear, though I did not fully understand it at the time.

The next day, I went searching. I visited several places without success until I walked into a Goodwill store. As I entered the furniture section, I immediately saw it, the exact piece I had seen inwardly. Without hesitation, I walked over, placed my hand on it, and said, "This is mine."

When I looked closer, I saw that it had already been claimed. I asked about it and was told the person would likely return for it. At that moment, I had an opportunity to pursue it further, but I walked away. Something in me hesitated.

Yet even as I left, I could not find peace. The thought of that piece would not leave me. Then, inwardly, I sensed the Holy Spirit speak: *"A businessman would go back and negotiate."*

That shifted everything. I returned to the store. This time, I pursued the matter differently. As events unfolded, the claim ticket was found unattended, the managers were called, and I was given the opportunity to purchase the piece immediately. The cost was minimal, far less than I expected.

As I walked away, I realized what had truly happened. The issue was never the rack. The lesson was obedience. I had seen it and claimed it, but I almost lost it because I hesitated. The Spirit had spoken clearly, but I allowed what I saw in the natural to override what I knew inwardly.

Yet the Holy Spirit did not abandon me. He remained persistent, guiding me back until I aligned with what had already been revealed. This is how the inward life works. The lesson was not about provision, but alignment.

When God speaks to the heart, it does not always align with what the senses perceive. The mind may question. The situation may contradict, but the inward witness remains steady. Learning to follow that voice requires trust, sensitivity, and sometimes correction.

God speaks to the heart, not as a metaphor, but as a person. The Spirit does not merely speak once. He leads, reminds, and draws us back until we learn to walk in agreement with Him.

Many assume that when Scripture refers to God speaking to the heart, it means feelings, impressions, or intuition. However, the heart is not merely emotional; it is spiritual. It is the hidden man of the heart, the place of direct communication between God and humanity.

At times, this inward communication becomes so clear that it cannot be mistaken. There have been moments in my life where this reality became unmistakably clear. On two occasions, while driving on Interstate

285 near Campbellton Road in Atlanta, I heard my name called clearly and audibly: *"Reggie."* The voice was so distinct that I immediately looked into the passenger seat, expecting to see someone there. There was no one. I looked into the surrounding lanes, thinking perhaps someone had called out from another vehicle. Again, there was no one. The voice had not come from the outside. It had come to me.

On another occasion, while driving in the same area, the voice of God spoke again, this time with clarity and conviction: *"Fornicators have no inheritance in the kingdom of God."* I did not fully understand the meaning of "inheritance," but I understood enough to know the seriousness of what was being said.

At another point in my life, while attending a church picnic at Grant Park, I was asked to come forward for prayer. I hesitated, not because I did not believe, but because I was concerned about how I would appear in front of some beautiful women. In that moment, God spoke again, this time more gently but no less clearly: *"If you are ashamed of me before men, I will be ashamed of you before my Father in heaven"* (Matthew 10:33). That settled the matter. I went forward.

These moments were not emotional impressions or passing thoughts. They were direct, clear, personal, and authoritative communications to the inward man of the heart. These moments are not the norm, but they reveal the clarity with which God is able to communicate when He chooses.

God speaks in ways that leave no confusion about the source. Sometimes His voice is strong and arresting. At other times, it is gentle but unmistakable. Yet in every case, it reaches beyond the surface of human reasoning and speaks directly to the spirit.

Scripture affirms this reality: *"For those who are led by the Spirit of God are the children of God"* (Romans 8:14). To be led by the Spirit is not to be governed by emotion, but to be guided by a living relationship with God through the inward man.

God does not speak to a concept. He speaks to a person, the hidden man of the heart. To love God with the heart begins here. It is not first expressed in outward action, but in inward response, the willingness of the hidden man to hear, trust, and yield to the voice of God.

The Fruit of the Spirit Within

If the hidden man of the heart is alive and aligned with God, then its nature will become visible. Scripture describes this through the fruit of the Spirit. The hidden man of the heart is not an abstract idea or a distant spiritual concept. Scripture presents the inward man as a living reality within the believer, shaped by relationship with God and expressed through character. The nature of this inward life can be understood through what Scripture calls the fruit of the Spirit.

Jesus described this relationship using the image of a vine and its branches. He said, "I am the vine, you are the branches. He who abides in me, and I in him, bears much fruit; for without me you can do nothing." This picture reveals that the life of the believer does not originate within the individual but flows from connection with Christ. The branch does not produce fruit by effort alone. It bears fruit because it remains connected to the source of life.

In the same way, the hidden man of the heart produces spiritual fruit as it abides in Christ. The apostle Paul identifies these qualities clearly: love, joy, peace, longsuffering, gentleness, goodness, faith, meekness, and temperance. These are not merely moral ideals to be imitated. They are the natural expression of a life that is connected to God.

These qualities appear first within the inward man before they are seen outwardly. The heart becomes the place where these attributes take root, and from there they begin to influence the soul and the body.

Love is the foundation of this inward life. It is not merely an emotion but a deliberate orientation toward others that reflects the nature of God. This love expresses itself in selflessness, willingness to sacrifice, and a commitment that is not dependent on circumstances. It mirrors the character of God, who is described in Scripture as love.

Joy follows as a response to confidence in God. It is not dependent on favorable circumstances but arises from trust in the promises of God. Even in difficulty, the inward man can remain anchored in the assurance that God is faithful to complete what He has begun.

Peace flows from the presence of God within the heart. It is a steady condition of the inner life that is not easily disturbed by external events. This peace reflects the order that comes when the spirit, soul, and body are aligned under the authority of God.

Longsuffering, or patience, expresses the ability to endure difficulty without losing stability or direction. It reflects God's own patience toward humanity and develops as the believer learns to trust His timing rather than demand immediate results.

Gentleness and goodness reveal how the inward life relates to others. Gentleness is strength expressed with restraint and wisdom, while goodness reflects a commitment to what is right and beneficial. Together they demonstrate the character of God in practical ways.

Faith, in this context, is not merely belief but a steady trust in God that shapes how the believer responds to life. It reflects confidence in the truth of God's Word and reliance upon His promises.

Meekness describes strength that is submitted to God. It is not weakness but controlled strength that does not seek to dominate others. It allows the believer to remain humble while standing firmly in truth.

Temperance, or self-control, represents the ability to govern one's desires and actions. It reflects a life that is no longer driven by impulse but directed by the Spirit of God.

These qualities together describe the nature of the hidden man of the heart. They are not produced through human effort alone but develop as the believer remains connected to Christ. As this inward life grows, its influence becomes visible. The soul begins to reflect these qualities in thought and emotion, and the body expresses them through action.

In this way the fruit of the Spirit provides clear evidence of the condition of the inner life. Where the hidden man is aligned with God, these qualities will increasingly appear. They serve as both a sign of spiritual life and a guide for continued growth.

The Diet of the Inward Man

Just as the body requires food to sustain physical life, the hidden man of the heart requires nourishment to sustain spiritual life. The inward man cannot thrive on natural provision alone. He must be fed by that which is spiritual, eternal, and life-giving.

Jesus revealed this truth plainly in the Gospel of John when He declared, *"I am the bread of life: he that cometh to me shall never hunger; and he that believeth on me shall never thirst"* (John 6:35). In this statement, He was not speaking of physical hunger but of a deeper need within the human being. The spirit of man longs for life, truth, and connection with God, and that need can only be satisfied in Christ.

This teaching became even more profound when Jesus said, *"My flesh is meat indeed, and my blood is drink indeed"* (John 6:55). Many who heard Him struggled to understand because the soul, through its natural reasoning, cannot fully grasp spiritual truth. Jesus clarified this by saying, *"It is the Spirit that gives life; the flesh profits nothing. The words that I speak unto you, they are spirit, and they are life"* (John 6:63).

The nourishment of the inward man is therefore not physical, but spiritual. It comes through receiving the Word of God, believing it, and living in alignment with it. Jesus Himself modeled this life when He said, *"My meat is to do the will of Him that sent me, and to finish His work"* (John 4:34). For Him, obedience to the Father was not a burden; it was sustenance.

This reveals a powerful truth. The inward man is strengthened not only by hearing the Word of God, but by walking in it. Spiritual nourishment is incomplete until truth becomes lived experience.

This nourishment is not limited to what is eaten, but also includes what is received as living water. Jesus spoke of this in the Gospel of John when He said, *"Whoever drinks of the water that I shall give him will never thirst; but the water that I shall give him will become in him a well of water springing up into everlasting life"* (John 4:14). In this statement, He reveals that the life of God is not only given to sustain, but to flow continuously within the believer.

This living water speaks of the presence and work of the Holy Spirit within the inward man. While the Word feeds and strengthens, the Spirit refreshes, renews, and brings continual life. The inward man is not sustained by occasional encounters with God, but by an ongoing, living connection in which spiritual life flows from within. In this way, the believer does not merely receive life from God but becomes a vessel through which that life continues to spring up, bringing renewal, clarity, and spiritual vitality.

The natural man seeks satisfaction in the pleasures of the world, such as the lust of the eyes, the lust of the flesh, and the pride of life (1 John 2:16). Yet these things cannot sustain the inward man. They leave the soul restless and unfulfilled. Only the Bread of Life can bring lasting satisfaction.

When the inward man is properly nourished, transformation begins to take place. The spirit becomes strong, the soul begins to come into order, and the body follows in obedience. The life of the believer then becomes aligned with the will of God from the inside out.

The diet of the inward man is therefore clear:

- the Word of God, which nourishes and strengthens
- the will of God, which sustains through obedience
- the life of Christ received by faith, which enables righteousness and transformation
- the living water of the Holy Spirit, which renews, fills and continually flows within

When these become the source of nourishment, the believer begins to experience the fullness of life that God intended from the beginning. The diet of the inward man is therefore complete in four dimensions. It is nourished by the Word of God, sustained through obedience to the will of God, anchored in the life of Christ received by faith, and continually refreshed by the living water of the Holy Spirit flowing within. Simply put, the inward man:

- eats (Word)
- acts (will)
- believes (faith)
- flows (Spirit)

The hidden man learns to trust the wisdom of the Creator, to listen for His direction, and to follow wherever He leads. This inward life becomes the foundation for everything else that follows, but understanding the hidden man of the heart also raises another important question: *If the spirit of man is the place where God communicates, what role does the soul play in human life?*

The soul, where thoughts, emotions, and decisions occur, stands between the spirit and thc body. It receives information from the world, processes these experiences, and determines how a person responds. We'll explore this further in PART II.

The Witness Within: The Role of Conscience

The hidden man of the heart does not operate in silence. One of the ways in which it expresses itself is through what Scripture describes as the conscience. The conscience is more than a feeling of guilt or approval. The conscience can be understood as the inward witness that responds when the spirit of man aligns with the Spirit of God, responding to truth and bearing testimony to what is right or wrong.

The writer of Hebrews speaks of hearts being "sprinkled to cleanse us from a guilty conscience" (Hebrews 10:22). This reveals that the conscience is not merely psychological but deeply spiritual. It is connected to the condition of the inward man. Before salvation, the conscience may be burdened, conflicted, or dulled by sin. After salvation, it is cleansed and brought into alignment with the truth of God.

In this sense, the conscience can be understood as the inward awareness that results when the spirit of man responds to the Spirit of God. The apostle Paul writes, "My conscience confirms it through the Holy Spirit" (Romans 9:1), indicating that the conscience does not function independently, but in relationship with God's Spirit.

This helps explain why the believer is called to maintain a clear conscience. A clear conscience is not the absence of awareness, but the result of alignment. It reflects a life in which the inward man is receiving truth from God, and the soul is responding in obedience. Peter writes of "a clear conscience toward God" (1 Peter 3:21), showing that this clarity is part of the believer's ongoing relationship with Him.

It is important, however, to distinguish between the voice of the conscience and the reasoning of the natural mind. The soul processes thoughts, emotions, and decisions, but the conscience bears witness to truth at a deeper level. When the soul is not aligned with the spirit, the conscience may be ignored, resisted, or overridden. When the soul is submitted, the conscience becomes a guide that confirms the direction of God.

For this reason, the believer must learn to recognize and respond to this inward witness. It is not a replacement for the Word of God, but it works in harmony with it. The same Spirit who inspired Scripture also bears witness within the heart. A life that is sensitive to the voice of the inward man is a life that remains open to the leading of God.

To say that a person has no conscience is, at minimum, to recognize that there is a broken relationship between that person's spirit and the Holy Spirit. The absence of that inner witness reflects a deeper disconnection from the source of truth. Conversely, to say that one's conscience is clear is to acknowledge that, in a given matter, the Holy Spirit has communicated with the hidden man of the heart. From there, the spirit directs the soul, and the soul in turn directs the body, bringing the whole person into alignment with what God has revealed.

The hidden man of the heart, therefore, is not passive. It hears, it receives, and it bears witness to truth. It is the place where God speaks and where His voice is first recognized. Yet hearing alone is not the end of the matter. What is received within the heart must be embraced, trusted, and established, for it is not enough to hear the voice of God. The heart must believe what it hears.

Chapter 5

Believing with the Heart

If the heart is the hidden spiritual person within us, then an important question naturally follows: **How does belief actually occur in the heart?**

The Scriptures repeatedly say that belief takes place in the heart. The apostle Paul writes:

> *"For with the heart man believeth unto righteousness; and with the mouth confession is made unto salvation."* (Romans 10:10)

At first glance this statement may seem simple, but it reveals a profound truth about the design of human life. Belief is not merely an intellectual activity that forms in the mind. This establishes something foundational: belief is not completed in the mind; it is *settled* in the heart. Thus, true faith originates in the inner spiritual person, the hidden man of the heart. To understand this process, we must first recognize how the different parts of human nature work together.

The Bible teaches that human beings are **tri-part in design**. A person is a spirit, possesses a soul, and lives in a body. Each of these dimensions participates in the process of belief, but they do not contribute equally. The body connects us with the physical world through our senses. The soul processes thoughts, emotions, and decisions. The spirit, or the deepest dimension of the hidden man of the heart, is the place where communion with God occurs.

Each of these parts plays a role in the process of belief. When a person hears the Word of God, the message is first received through the senses of the body. The ears hear the spoken word. The eyes may read the Scriptures. These physical senses act as gateways through which information enters human experience.

Once information enters through the senses, it is processed by the soul. The soul includes the mind, emotions, and will. The mind considers the message, evaluates it, and reflects on its meaning. The emotions respond to the message with feelings such as hope, curiosity, resistance, or conviction. Finally, the will decides whether to accept or reject what has been heard. However, the soul does not complete the process.

After the soul receives and evaluates the message, the conclusion it reaches is presented to the heart, the hidden man within. It is in this inward place that belief is either embraced or rejected. When the heart receives the Word of God with faith, something remarkable happens. The spirit of man begins to interact with the Spirit of God. This interaction is the foundation of spiritual life.

Jesus illustrated this process when He spoke about faith in the Gospel of Mark. After the disciples observed the withered fig tree, Jesus said:

> *"Have faith in God... Truly I tell you, if anyone says to this mountain, 'Go, throw yourself into the sea,' and does not doubt in their heart but believes what they say will happen, it will be done for them."* (Mark 11:22–23)

Notice that Jesus did not say belief must occur in the mind. Instead,

He emphasized belief in the heart. This distinction matters because the mind may understand a concept intellectually while the heart remains unconvinced. A person may comprehend that something is possible while still harboring doubt within the inward man. This explains why understanding alone does not produce faith.

Faith becomes effective when the heart fully embraces the truth of God's Word. Once belief takes root in the heart, it begins to influence the rest of the person. The soul becomes aligned with what the spirit believes. Thoughts begin to change. Emotions begin to shift. Decisions begin to reflect the new conviction.

Finally, the body expresses what the heart believes through speech and action. This is why Scripture links belief in the heart with confession through the mouth. The mouth does not create faith; it reveals what has already been established within the heart.

In this way, the entire person becomes involved in the process of faith. Seen together, the process of belief unfolds in a clear progression: The body hears the Word. The soul considers the Word. The heart believes the Word. The mouth confesses the Word.

This pattern reflects the design God placed within human beings. However, the process can also work in the opposite direction. When the soul rejects the Word of God, doubt begins to dominate the heart. Fear, reasoning, and imagination can weaken faith before it has a chance to take root. This is why Scripture warns believers to guard the heart carefully. The information that enters the mind influences what the heart eventually believes.

The eyes see. The ears hear. The mind processes. The heart decides.

For this reason, the condition of the heart must be continually strengthened through exposure to the Word of God. The apostle Paul explains this principle when he writes: *"Faith comes by hearing, and hearing by the word of God."* (Romans 10:17). As a person repeatedly hears and meditates on God's Word, the heart becomes increasingly convinced of its truth. What begins as understanding in the mind gradually becomes conviction in the spirit. When this transformation occurs, faith moves from theory to reality.

The hidden man of the heart begins to live in confidence toward God. Fear and doubt lose their control. The believer learns to trust the promises of God even when circumstances appear uncertain. This kind of faith does not originate from human effort alone. It grows out of a relationship with God in which the heart learns to listen for His voice and respond in obedience. In this way, believing with the heart is inseparable from loving God with the heart. Love is not merely emotion; it is trust. It is the inward agreement of the heart with what God has said.

Over time the inward man becomes stronger and more sensitive to the leading of the Holy Spirit. However, this raises another important question. If the heart is the place where belief occurs and the spirit is the part of human nature that communes with God, **what role does the soul play in shaping daily life?**

The soul stands between the spirit and the body. It is the place where thoughts are formed, emotions are experienced, and choices are made. When the soul aligns itself with the spirit, the entire person begins to live in harmony with God. This reveals something that must be clearly understood: belief does not originate at the level of thought alone.

Belief Beyond the Mind

One of the most important questions in the life of faith is where belief actually occurs. Many people assume that belief is primarily an activity of the mind. They associate belief with agreement, reasoning or intellectual understanding. While the mind plays a role in processing information, Scripture points to a deeper place where belief is formed.

Jesus spoke about this when He said that whoever believes in his heart and does not doubt will see what he says come to pass. This statement directs attention away from surface-level thinking and toward the inward man. Belief, in its fullest sense, does not originate in the intellect alone. It takes root within the hidden man of the heart.

The distinction is important. A person may agree with truth mentally and yet remain unchanged inwardly. True belief involves more than acknowledgment. It involves internal conviction that shapes how a person thinks, speaks, and lives.

It is possible to know something without truly believing it. Knowledge can exist at the level of the mind without reaching the depth of the heart. A person may understand what Scripture teaches and even agree with it yet still struggle to live in alignment with that truth.

This gap between knowing and believing often becomes evident in moments of pressure. When circumstances become difficult, the mind may recall what is true, but the heart reveals what is actually believed. Fear, doubt, or hesitation can expose areas where belief has not yet taken root.

Scripture consistently calls believers beyond knowledge into conviction. Belief in the heart produces stability because it is not easily shaken by changing circumstances. It becomes a settled reality within the inward man.

The Role of the Soul in Belief

The soul plays an important role in the process of belief. It receives information, processes experiences, and forms interpretations about life. Thoughts, emotions, and reasoning all pass through the soul. However, the soul itself does not determine final belief. It influences the process but does not complete it. Because of this, the condition of the soul can either support or resist what the spirit receives.

The information processed in the soul is presented to the heart, where it is either accepted or rejected. This explains why two people can hear the same truth and respond differently. The difference lies not in what was heard but in what was received within the heart.

The condition of the soul can influence this process. Fear, pride, or emotional attachment may resist truth before it reaches the heart. Thus, the renewal of the mind (Chapter 10) becomes essential, as it prepares the soul to align with what the Spirit reveals.

Belief and Confession

Once belief is established in the heart, it does not remain hidden. Jesus connected belief in the heart with the words that a person speaks. He taught that when a person believes without doubting, what they say will reflect that belief. Speech becomes an outward expression of inward conviction. This is why Scripture consistently links belief with confession.

This connection reveals that belief is not passive. It produces expression. What fills the heart eventually comes out through words and actions. When belief is rooted in truth, the words of a person begin to align with that truth.

This principle also explains why inconsistent speech often reflects inconsistent belief. A person may speak faith in one moment and doubt in another. These fluctuations point to areas where belief has not yet become settled within the heart.

The Power of Belief

Belief does not always develop instantly. It grows as the believer is exposed to truth and responds to it consistently. As the Word is received, considered, and embraced, belief begins to take shape within the heart. This process requires more than repeated exposure to information. It involves yielding to truth. The heart must allow what is heard to take root. Over time, truth moves from being something understood to something lived.

As belief develops, it produces confidence. The inward man becomes anchored in what God has said. This confidence is not based on circumstances but on the reliability of God's Word.

Belief in the heart carries real spiritual consequence. Jesus taught that what a person believes without doubt has the power to shape outcomes (Mark 9:23). This does not suggest that belief is a tool for controlling circumstances according to personal desire. Rather, it reveals that belief aligns the individual with the purposes of God. It does not create reality independently, but brings the believer into agreement with what God has established.

When the heart is aligned with God's truth, the believer begins to participate in what God is doing. Prayer becomes more than request. It becomes agreement. Speech becomes more than expression. It becomes declaration of what is believed.

In this way, belief functions as a bridge between the unseen and the seen. What is established in the heart begins to influence what is experienced in life.

Guarding the Heart in Belief

Because belief is formed in the heart, Scripture emphasizes the importance of guarding it. Thoughts, experiences, affiliations, and influences all contribute to the formation of belief. What a person allows into the inner life will influence what is believed, so it must be carefully managed.

Guarding the heart does not mean withdrawing from life but becoming intentional about what is received and embraced. Truth must be allowed to take root, while deception must be resisted.

As the heart is guarded and nourished with truth, belief becomes stronger and more consistent. The inward man becomes stable, and the life of the believer begins to reflect that stability.

The Movement of Faith: Hearing, Believing, Acting

This process can also be understood more simply as *hearing, believing,* and *acting*. It is an active process through which the Word of God moves from hearing into conviction and ultimately into action. Faith begins when the Word is received, but it does not remain complete until it is acted upon. The process can be understood in three movements: hearing, believing, and acting.

Hearing is the entry point. The Word of God must first be received, whether through reading, teaching, or proclamation. This is not merely the reception of information, but the introduction of divine truth into the inward man. The spirit hears beyond the natural ear, and something deeper begins to respond.

As the Word is received, it moves inward and becomes conviction in the heart. This is where faith is formed. Jesus emphasized this when He said, *"Whoever says to this mountain, 'Be removed and be cast into the sea,' and does not doubt in his heart but believes that those things he says will come to pass, he will have whatever he says"* (Mark 11:23). The heart becomes the place where truth is either accepted or rejected.

Acting is the outward expression of what has been believed. Faith does not remain hidden within the heart. It reveals itself through obedience, confession, and response. James writes, *"Faith without works is dead"* (James 2:17), showing that genuine belief will always produce corresponding action.

This pattern is especially evident in matters of healing. Scripture declares that provision has already been made through Christ. As written by the prophet Isaiah, *"By his stripes we are healed"* (Isaiah 53:5), a truth later affirmed in the New Testament (1 Peter 2:24). Yet this provision must be received through faith.

The believer hears the Word concerning healing, believes it within the heart, and then acts in alignment with that belief. This action may take the form of prayer, confession or obedience to the leading of the

Spirit. In each case, faith moves from inward conviction to outward expression. This reveals an important truth. Faith is not merely agreement with Scripture. It is participation in it.

As the believer continues in this pattern – hearing the Word, believing it in the heart, and acting upon it – confidence grows. What once required effort begins to flow more naturally. The soul learns to trust what the spirit has received, and the life of faith becomes increasingly consistent.

Believing with the heart is not a single moment but a way of living. It is the continual response of the inward man to the Word of God, resulting in a life that reflects His truth in real and tangible ways. When belief takes root within the heart, the soul aligns, the body follows, and the whole person begins to live from the inside out. Thus, believing with the heart ultimately shapes how a person lives. The inward conviction formed within the hidden man influences the soul and directs the body. When thoughts align with belief, actions follow conviction, and life begins to reflect what is held within. This is why Scripture places such emphasis on the heart. It is the source from which life flows. When the heart believes rightly, the rest of life begins to come into alignment. This is the life of faith, an inward conviction shaping outward reality.

The call to believe with the heart is, therefore, a call to live from the inside out. It is an invitation to allow truth to take root in the deepest part of one's being so that every aspect of life is shaped by it. Understanding how this alignment takes place is essential for understanding the spiritual life.

In the next part (II), we will look more closely at the soul and examine why it often becomes the place of greatest inner tension in the life of faith.

PART II – THE SOUL

The Inner Life and the Battle of the Mind

Chapter 6

What Is the Soul

If the heart is the hidden spiritual person within us, then the next question naturally arises: **what is the soul?**

Belief is formed in the heart, and the soul is where that belief is processed, tested, and lived out. However, many people use the words *heart* and *soul* interchangeably. In everyday speech, someone may say, "I love you with all my heart and soul," without thinking about whether those two words describe the same thing or different aspects of human life.

People often speak of "soulmates," "soul searching." Music, poetry, and literature frequently use the word *soul* to describe the deepest part of a person. Yet, in many cases, the word is used without a clear understanding of what it truly means.

Scripture does not treat the soul as a vague or poetic idea. The Bible speaks of the soul with precision and consistency, revealing that it is central to human identity. When God created man, He did not simply form a body or impart a spirit. The book of Genesis states:

> *"And the Lord God formed man of the dust of the ground, and breathed into his nostrils the breath of life; and man became a living soul"* (Genesis 2:7).

This statement reveals that the soul is not an abstract idea, but the conscious life of the person, the point at which existence becomes experience. This understanding is reinforced in other parts of Scripture. The apostle Paul writes:

> *"May your whole spirit, soul and body be preserved blameless unto the coming of our Lord Jesus Christ"* (1 Thessalonians 5:23).

The writer of Hebrews declares: *"For the word of God is living and active... it penetrates even to dividing soul and spirit"* (Hebrews 4:12). Together, these passages reveal two important truths. First, human beings are tri-part in nature: spirit, soul, and body. Second, the soul and the spirit are not the same. They are distinct, though closely related.

A person is a spirit, possesses a soul, and lives in a body. Each of these dimensions plays a different role in the experience of life.

- The **body** connects us with the physical world. Through the senses we see, hear, taste, smell, and touch. The body allows us to interact with the environment around us.
- The **spirit**, the hidden man of the heart, connects us with God. It is the place where faith is born, where the voice of God is heard, and where communion with the Creator takes place.
- Between these two lies the **soul**, the inner life of the person. It includes the mind, emotions, and will, the faculties through which a person thinks, feels, and makes decisions. Through the soul, we become aware of ourselves, others, and our surroundings.

While the spirit receives from God and the body expresses outwardly, the soul stands between them as the place where life is interpreted and decisions are made. The soul, however, must not be reduced to a set of functions or faculties. The soul is the conscious dimension of the person, the place where thought, emotion, and choice are experienced.

The mind, emotions, and will are not separate from the soul; they are expressions of the soul. They are how the soul processes life. Through the mind, the soul thinks and reasons. Through the emotions, it experiences joy, sorrow, fear, and desire. Through the will, it makes decisions and acts. Behind all of these is the soul itself: the "you" who lives within the body.

When two people speak to one another, they are not merely interacting with physical bodies. They are engaging with each other as living souls. The eyes see, the ears hear, and the voice speaks, but it is the soul that perceives, understands, and responds. The body serves as the outward vessel, but the soul is the inward life through which a person becomes conscious of thought, emotion, and choice.

Understanding this distinction is essential. Many define the soul as the mind, emotions, and will, as though it were simply a collection of parts. Scripture presents something deeper. The soul is not a system of functions; it is the conscious dimension of the person through which life is experienced and expressed.

It is within this inward life that decisions are made, attachments are formed, and responses to truth are shaped. It is this same conscious life that will stand before God, give account, and continue beyond physical death either in His presence or apart from Him.

The Spirit and the Soul

The soul is where life is experienced, but it is not the deepest source of life itself. It exists in close relationship with the spirit. The spirit of man, like the soul, is not imaginary or symbolic. It is a real dimension of human existence, designed specifically for communion with God.

A helpful way to understand their distinction is this: with his spirit, man is *God-conscious*; with his soul, he is *self-conscious*; and with his body, he is *world-conscious.* The spirit is oriented toward God. It receives from Him, responds to Him, and is the place where faith is born. The soul, on the other hand, is aware of itself. It evaluates, reasons, feels, and chooses. It is through the soul that a person becomes aware of identity, relationships, and experience. This distinction explains why the soul can be active and expressive while still being misaligned with God.

Because of this, the soul often becomes the most active, dominant part of human life, and therefore, the most influential in daily living. It is constantly processing information, reacting to circumstances, and forming conclusions. Yet Scripture reveals that the soul was never intended to lead independently of the spirit. It was designed to be guided by it.

When the soul submits to the spirit, life begins to align with God's design. The spirit receives direction from God, and the soul responds by bringing thoughts, emotions, and decisions into agreement with that direction. The result is clarity, stability, and spiritual growth.

However, when the soul operates apart from the spirit, disorder often follows. The mind begins to rely solely on human reasoning. Emotions fluctuate according to circumstances. The will pursues personal desires rather than divine direction. In this state, the soul attempts to lead without reference to God.

This creates an internal conflict. A person may sense what is right within the spirit yet feel resistance within the soul. This tension is the battlefield of the inner life. The mind questions what the spirit knows. This is the tension of the inner life, the place where faith is either strengthened or resisted. Emotions react with fear or uncertainty. The will hesitates to surrender control. This tension explains why spiritual growth is often accompanied by struggle.

The Word of God plays a crucial role in this process, exposing the difference between what is revealed by the spirit and what is produced by the soul. Hebrews teaches that it is able to divide between soul and spirit (Hebrews 4:12). This does not mean that the two are enemies, but that they are distinct. The Word reveals what originates from the soul and what originates from the spirit, helping the believer discern truth from reaction.

If the heart is the place where faith is born, then the soul is the place where that faith is lived out. Faith, or obedience, is how we express our love to God (John 14:15). To love God with the soul is to bring the mind, emotions, and will into agreement with what the heart receives from God. This is where love becomes visible in thought, feeling, and decision, but it is often where the greatest struggle occurs. The mind may question, the emotions may resist, and the will may hesitate. Yet love for God is not complete until the soul yields to the truth received within the spirit.

As the soul learns to align with the spirit, thoughts become clearer, emotions become steadier, and decisions begin to reflect trust in God rather than reaction to circumstances.

The Nature of the Soul

To understand why struggle exists, we must consider the natural tendencies of the soul. The soul is the seat of self-awareness. It is where identity is experienced and expressed. It is also where attachments are formed, desires are cultivated, and decisions are made. Thus, by its nature, the soul tends toward independence, preferring to interpret life on its own terms rather than submit to what is received from God. It evaluates life based on what it sees, feels, and understands. It seeks control and often prefers to rely on its own reasoning. This tendency can lead the soul to resist the direction of the spirit, especially when that direction requires trust beyond what is immediately visible.

Because the soul is the center of thought, emotion, and will, it is also the place where conflict is most deeply experienced. Fear, doubt, imagination, and desire all operate within the soul. These influences can either align with truth or oppose it.

Spiritual growth, therefore, involves the transformation of the soul. The mind must be renewed by truth. The emotions must be brought into stability. The will must learn to yield to God. As this transformation takes place, the soul becomes increasingly aligned with the spirit.

Soul Attachments

The influence of the soul can be seen clearly in the way attachments form and shape decision-making. There was a time in my younger years when I experienced this firsthand.

I had arranged to meet a young woman at her home one evening. When I arrived, I knocked on the door and waited, but there was no response. After knocking several times, I stepped back and noticed through the window that she was inside, lying on the sofa and talking on the telephone. When I knocked again, she quickly got up, moved out of sight, and then came to the door as though nothing had happened.

When I asked her about it, she denied being on the phone, even when I asked her directly while looking into her eyes. The moment was confusing, because what I had seen was clear, yet what I heard contradicted it. Despite recognizing the inconsistency, I did not walk away from the relationship.

Looking back, the reason becomes clear. My judgment had been influenced by attachment within the soul. Emotional connection can bind a person in ways that override logic and evidence. The soul can hold on even when the mind recognizes that something is wrong. What I experienced was not confusion of facts, but conflict within the soul.

This helps explain why people often remain in situations that bring confusion or pain. They may say, "I know I should leave, but I cannot," or "My mind says one thing, but my heart says another." These statements reflect the tension within the soul, where thoughts, emotions, and desires may not be in agreement.

The soul has the capacity to form deep attachments, and those attachments can influence perception, decision-making, and behavior. When the soul is governed primarily by emotion or desire, it may resist truth. Learning to recognize this influence is essential for bringing the soul into alignment with God.

The Soul in Transformation

Because the soul is not naturally aligned with the spirit, it must be transformed. In fact, the transformation of the soul is one of the most important aspects of the spiritual life. As the soul learns to trust the guidance of the spirit and the truth of God's Word, it begins to change. The mind becomes renewed, learning to think in agreement with truth rather than assumption. The emotions become steadier, no longer controlled by circumstance alone. The will becomes surrendered, choosing obedience over independence and trust over control

When this alignment takes place, the soul no longer resists the spirit but cooperates with it. The result is a life that reflects harmony between the inner and outer dimensions of a person. This transformation does not happen instantly, nor does it occur without resistance. The soul often becomes the place where fear, doubt, and imagination attempt to challenge what the spirit has received from God. Yet as the soul yields, it becomes increasingly aligned with divine purpose.

Understanding the soul in this way provides a foundation for the chapter that follows. The next step is to explore how the soul comes under the leadership of the spirit and what happens when that alignment is established.

Chapter 7

The Soul Under the Spirit

If the soul is the dimension where thoughts, emotions, and decisions occur, then a critical question must be asked: **Who should lead the soul?** The answer to this question determines the direction of a person's life, for **if the soul processes life, then its direction determines the course of that life.**

When God created humanity, He designed human life to operate in a specific order. The spirit, or the deepest dimension of the hidden man of the heart, was meant to live in communion with God. The soul was meant to receive guidance from the spirit. The body was meant to carry out the actions that resulted from those inward decisions.

In this design the spirit leads, the soul cooperates, and the body expresses what the inner life has determined. When this order is preserved, life begins to function in harmony. More importantly, this is the order in which love for God becomes fully expressed – from inward communion to outward obedience.

Disrupting Divine Alignment

The spirit hears the voice of God. The soul receives that guidance and aligns with it. The body acts in obedience. In this way the entire person becomes aligned with the purposes of God.

However, human life does not always function according to this design. Because the soul possesses the ability to think, reason, and choose, it often attempts to guide life independently of the spirit. The mind may rely on human reasoning rather than spiritual wisdom. Emotions may react to circumstances with fear or anxiety. The will may seek control rather than surrender.

When this happens, the natural order of life becomes reversed. Instead of the spirit leading, the soul attempts to lead life apart from the guidance of the spirit. The mind begins to dominate the inner life. Emotions rise and fall with circumstances. Decisions are made based on personal preference rather than divine guidance. Basically, when the soul leads, life becomes reaction-driven. When the spirit leads, life becomes truth-driven.

This reversal creates inner instability. The spirit may sense the direction of God, while the soul hesitates to follow. The mind may question what the spirit knows. Emotions may resist the path that faith requires. The will may struggle to surrender control. This tension explains why many believers experience an internal battle between what they know spiritually and what they feel emotionally.

Paul and the other apostles described the conflict between the inward desire to follow God and the opposing influences within human nature (Romans 6:19; Galatians 5:17; James 4:1; 1 Peter 2:11). Scripture often describes spiritual conflict using the term "the flesh." The flesh is not merely the physical body and its desires, nor does it refer to the entire being. It describes the nature of human life when it operates apart from the guidance of the spirit. In this state, the soul, through its thoughts, emotions, and desires, aligns itself with what is natural rather than what is revealed by God. Essentially, the flesh is a misaligned soul expressing itself through the body.

This is why the apostle Paul writes that "the flesh desires what is contrary to the Spirit, and the Spirit what is contrary to the flesh" (Gal. 5:17). The conflict is not simply physical, but internal. It is the tension between a life directed by self and a life directed by God. When the soul follows its own reasoning and desires, it resists the direction of the spirit. When it yields to the spirit, it comes into alignment with the Spirit of God.

Spiritual growth often involves learning how to bring the soul into alignment with the spirit. The process begins with the renewal of the mind (Chapter 9). When the mind is exposed to the Word of God, it gradually begins to adopt a new perspective. Thoughts that once dominated the soul begin to lose their influence. Fear begins to give way to faith. Doubt begins to give way to trust.

The mind learns to recognize the voice of the spirit. As the mind changes, the emotions also begin to stabilize. Feelings that once controlled decisions begin to fall into proper order. Instead of reacting impulsively to circumstances, the soul learns to respond with wisdom and restraint.

The will, the decision-making faculty of the soul, also undergoes transformation. Rather than insisting on personal control, the will learns to submit to the direction of the spirit. This transformation is not instantaneous. It occurs gradually as the believer continues to grow in relationship with God.

The hidden man of the heart receives guidance from the Holy Spirit.

The soul learns to trust that guidance. The will chooses to obey what the spirit has received. Over time the soul becomes increasingly aligned with the spirit.

This alignment produces remarkable stability within the believer. The mind becomes clearer. Emotions become more disciplined. Decisions become more consistent with the character and purposes of God. Instead of being driven by fear, impulse, or circumstance, the soul begins to operate under spiritual leadership.

This does not mean the soul loses its individuality or personality. Rather, the soul finds its proper place within the design God intended. Thoughts, emotions, and decisions continue to function, but they do so under the guidance of the spirit rather than in opposition to it. The result is a life that reflects both spiritual wisdom and human expression.

When the soul submits to the spirit, the believer begins to experience greater peace and clarity. Inner conflict diminishes because the different parts of the person are no longer competing for control. Thus, the spirit leads, the soul cooperates, and the body obeys. In this alignment, the believer begins to live as God intended – from the inside out.

Yet even as the soul learns to submit to the spirit, another challenge often emerges. The mind can still become a place where fear, doubt, and imagination attempt to challenge the truth that the spirit has received. These internal struggles can become powerful obstacles if they are not understood properly.

Confronting the Fear of Death

One of the clearest places spiritual conflict appears is in the presence of fear. Among the deepest fears that can rise within the soul is the fear of death. Death represents helplessness, loss, finality, and separation, and for that reason it holds unusual power over the human imagination. Even believers who trust God may find that the thought of death stirs uneasiness within the mind and emotions. The soul recoils from what it cannot control, and death appears to be the ultimate loss of control.

Yet the gospel teaches that death does not hold ultimate authority over the child of God. Through Christ, its power has been broken. This truth does not mean that the soul never feels fear. It means that fear does not have the final word when the spirit is anchored in truth. The soul may tremble, but the spirit can still receive instruction from the Holy Spirit and respond in faith.

I experienced this reality in a vivid way during a season when I was renting a house and became aware of a dark spiritual presence entering the home. As I lay in bed, I sensed what I can only describe as a spirit of death moving toward me. The experience was not abstract. It felt personal, oppressive, and deliberate. My first response was to use every method of resistance I had learned. I tried to speak in tongues. I tried to rebuke the presence. I tried to force words out with strength and urgency. Yet nothing seemed to work, and as I struggled, the presence kept drawing closer.

What made the moment so revealing was not only the presence itself but the condition of my own soul. Fear pressed in, and the soul wanted to react through effort, volume, and panic. In that moment, however, the Holy Spirit spoke quietly to my spirit and said, "Just say Jesus."

The instruction was striking in its simplicity. It was not about effort, but about trust. I stopped striving and quietly said, "Jesus, Jesus, Jesus."

As I spoke His name, the dark presence stopped immediately. Then it turned and fled the way it had come, moving back down the hallway, through the kitchen, out the back door, and into the darkness beyond the house.

That experience taught me something important about the conflict within the soul. In moments of fear, the soul often assumes that more effort, more noise, or more human force is the answer. The Spirit of God, however, does not always lead through strain. Sometimes He leads through simple faith expressed in obedience. The power in that moment was not in my emotional intensity. The power was in the authority of Jesus' name and in yielding to the Spirit's instruction. What the soul tried to solve through intensity, the spirit resolved through obedience.

This is why the soul must learn to trust the spirit when fear arises. The mind may race, the emotions may tighten, and the imagination may magnify the threat. Even so, the spirit can still hear clearly from God. When the soul submits to that inward guidance instead of reacting to fear, peace begins to replace panic. The believer is reminded that darkness does not rule the inward life of the one who belongs to Christ. Fear may approach, but it does not own the soul that has learned to rest under the authority of Jesus.

For that reason, growth in this area is not merely about becoming less emotional or more courageous by natural temperament. It is about training the soul to respond to spiritual truth. The fear of death is real to the human soul, yet Christ has removed its final claim over those who belong to Him. The soul must therefore be renewed until it learns to stand in the confidence of what the spirit already knows: death is not master, fear is not lord, and the name of Jesus still carries authority.

Personal Glimpse of the Transition

While Scripture provides the foundation for understanding the soul, there are moments when that reality becomes deeply personal. There was a moment in my life when the reality of the soul became more than something I understood from Scripture. It became something I experienced. I had what I can only describe as an "open vision," a moment in which the natural and spiritual seemed to intersect while I was fully awake. It was accompanied by a discerning of spirits.

I was standing in my bedroom after studying when, without warning, I became aware that I was transitioning from this world. It felt as though I was being enveloped, drawn upward, almost like being lifted out of the natural realm. At the same time, I saw my physical body fall to the floor, clothes included, as though I had stepped out of it. They lay there in a heap, empty, while I remained fully aware.

There was no confusion or fear, only peace, silence, and the presence of God. I remember saying, "Okay, Father," as I became aware that I was preparing to depart. As I focused on this transition, I felt a deep sense of sadness, not fear, but the emotional weight of leaving behind those I love, especially my god-daughter and best friend. It was not fear of where I was going; it was the weight of what I was leaving behind. The feeling was immediate and intense, as though it hit me like a blow. My heart dropped deep within me. I knew how much they loved me, and I felt the depth of that love in that moment.

A single thought pressed into my awareness: *How would they know I was gone?* There was neither a time to call nor an opportunity to explain. The moment was moving forward, and I understood clearly that I could not stop it. That realization revealed something profound to me. The soul does not lose its capacity to love, feel or care. Even in the presence of God, those connections remained real. Yet even in that moment, there was a readiness, a peace in yielding to God.

Then something remarkable happened. Without turning my head, I became aware of another presence standing slightly behind me to my right. When I perceived it, I realized I was looking at myself. It was my soul, the conscious expression of my inward life – distinct, aware, and present. He appeared as I am: same height, build and features, though slightly different in complexion. There was no hair, no eyelashes, yet it was unmistakably me. He was not reacting emotionally, but he was aware, observant, and focused. He was watching.

As I stood there in that moment, fully aware, another understanding began to unfold. The Lord brought to my remembrance an experience I had previously encountered in a dream. In that dream, I opened the casket of a dead person. The moment it opened, an overwhelming stench rushed out with such force that it was impossible to ignore. The thick, penetrating, almost unbearable stench filled the space instantly. There was no mistaking it. It was the smell of death.

In this open vision, the Lord made the connection clear to me: this is how sin is perceived in His presence. It literally stinks from death, not only the sin of those who do not know Him, but any disobedience or condition of the soul that is out of alignment with Him. What may seem hidden, justified, or even small in the mind carries a reality before God that is altogether different. Thus, sin is not merely an action. It produces a condition within the soul itself, and that condition, apart from cleansing, carries the stench of death.

This revelation did not come with condemnation, but with clarity. It revealed both the seriousness of disobedience and the holiness of God. At the same time, it deepened my understanding of the necessity of cleansing. Because if the soul can carry the weight of that condition, then it must also be restored from it.

This is why the work of Christ is not optional. Through Him, what carries the residue of death can be made clean. What is offensive in the presence of God can be purified. The soul, though fully alive and aware, must also be brought into consecration before the holy God.

Ultimately, I understood something that cannot be easily explained: I was engaging with God, spirit to Spirit, while my soul stood present, distinct, and aware, observing the interaction. The experience was brief, but it left a lasting imprint on me. I came away with a deeper understanding that the soul is not abstract. It is not symbolic. It is the living person.

Since that moment, I have also become more intentional about staying connected to those I love. I find myself reaching out more, calling more often, making sure that what matters most is not left unsaid. Thus, the experience did not only reveal the reality of the soul. It revealed the value of relationships while we are still here.

In that moment, fear of death had no place. The presence of God removed it entirely. What many imagine as frightening was, in reality, peaceful. The transition was not chaotic or uncertain. It was immediate and purposeful.

This brought new clarity to the words of the apostle Paul:

> *"We are confident, I say, and willing rather to be absent from the body, and to be present with the Lord"* (2 Corinthians 5:8).

The soul does not wander. It does not linger. It transitions, and it remains fully alive. This reality is confirmed in Scripture.

The Transition Beyond the Body

One of the clearest revelations of the soul as a living being appears in the words of Jesus in the Gospel of Luke. Jesus tells the account of a rich man and a beggar named Lazarus (Luke 16:19–31). Both men died, yet the narrative does not describe them as unconscious or nonexistent. Instead, it presents them as fully aware, conscious, and recognizable.

The rich man lifts up his eyes in torment. He speaks. He remembers his life. He expresses concern for his brothers. Lazarus is comforted. Abraham speaks. There is awareness, identity, memory, and communication.

What is seen in this passage is not the activity of bodies, for the bodies had been buried. What remains active is the soul.

This moment may be described as the transition: the separation of the soul from the physical body. The outward body returns to the earth, but the inward person continues. The soul does not cease to exist. It continues in full awareness. This passage removes all ambiguity. The soul is not an abstract idea or a symbolic concept. It is the conscious life that continues beyond physical death.

Understanding this changes how we view life. The decisions made in time are carried by the soul into eternity. The soul that believes, chooses, and responds in this life is the same soul that stands before God. For this reason, the condition of the soul is of eternal importance.

There are moments in Scripture where Jesus speaks in a way that challenges human interpretation. One such moment occurs when He takes the bread and says, "This is my body," and the cup, saying, "This is my blood" (Luke 22:19–20).

Many have understood these words symbolically, as representation. Yet Jesus did not say this represents my body. He said, this is my body. This distinction is important. It reveals that spiritual reality is not always defined by outward appearance. What appears unchanged to the natural eye may carry a deeper reality in the spirit.

In a similar way, the soul is often treated as a concept or a collection of functions. Yet Scripture does not present the soul as a representation of the person. The soul is the conscious life of the person that continues beyond the body, which returns to the earth, but the inward life continues in full awareness.

Just as the bread remains visible while carrying a deeper meaning, the human body is visible while housing a living soul. The outward form may be seen, but the true conscious life is within.

A Soul Out of Alignment

The account of the rich man reveals something that is often misunderstood. The soul does not suddenly become aware after death. It is already living in a condition that will either continue in peace or in torment.

It is never my intent to make light of such a serious matter. However, the words of the rich man in the Gospel of Luke make one thing unmistakably clear: he was not resting in peace (Luke 16:23–24). His soul was fully aware, fully conscious, and fully engaged in the reality of his condition.

Hell, therefore, must be understood in two ways, as both a future reality and a present condition of separation. Scripture reveals it as a real place, yet it also reflects a condition that can begin within the soul even before physical death. A soul that is separated from God, governed by sin, and resistant to truth experiences a form of unrest that points toward that final separation.

This truth became personal to me on August 13, 1978. As I knelt in repentance in my bathtub, I found myself saying, "*I am back... what took me so long to return?*" In that moment, the Spirit of God spoke clearly within me: "*You've been living in hell all this time.*" That statement brought immediate clarity. A life marked by deception, immorality, and confusion had produced a condition within my soul that was far from the peace of God. The condition of my soul had reflected separation long before any final judgment.

The Lord is patient, not willing that any should perish but that all should come to repentance (2 Peter 3:9). That patience is an invitation. It reveals that the condition of the soul can change before its final destination is sealed.

The soul was never created to live apart from God. When it does, it experiences disorder, unrest, and separation. When it comes under the influence of the spirit and the truth of God's Word, it begins to experience restoration, peace, and alignment.

In the next chapter, we will examine the conflict within the soul and explore how fear, doubt, and imagination attempt to challenge the truth that the spirit has received from God.

Chapter 8

The Conflict Within the Soul

Even when the spirit is aligned with God, the soul does not always immediately follow. This reveals an important truth: alignment in the spirit does not automatically produce alignment in the soul. The hidden man of the heart may receive truth from the Word of God, yet the mind may question it. The spirit may sense direction from God, yet emotions may react with fear or uncertainty. The will may hesitate to act even when the heart believes. This tension within the soul is one of the most common experiences in the life of a believer.

The Battle for the Soul

To understand why this tension exists, we must recognize where the conflict takes place. The soul occupies a unique place in the life of every human being. It is the seat of self-awareness, the place where thoughts, emotions, desires, and choices converge. Because of this central role, the soul often becomes the arena in which the most significant struggles of life occur. It's where competing influences attempt to determine direction. Decisions are weighed there, fears take shape there, and the direction of life is frequently determined by what happens within the soul.

Scripture teaches that this inner conflict is not merely the result of human psychology or circumstance. The Bible describes a larger spiritual reality in which unseen influences seek to shape the thoughts and desires of the human heart. This is not only a psychological or emotional struggle; it is a spiritual one. From the earliest pages of Scripture to the teachings of Jesus and the apostles, the struggle for human allegiance appears as an ongoing contest between truth and deception, faith and doubt, obedience and rebellion.

For this reason, the soul often experiences tension between competing influences. The spirit within a believer longs to follow the direction of God, yet the soul may struggle with fear, pride, attachment, or uncertainty. These internal conflicts can manifest in many ways, such as through anxious thoughts, emotional turmoil, or the temptation to trust in something other than God. What appears to be a purely personal struggle may in fact reflect a deeper spiritual contest for the direction of the soul.

Scripture often describes this internal struggle as a conflict between the flesh and the Spirit. The flesh refers to the natural human life as it operates through the body and the desires that arise within the soul when they are not governed by the spirit. For this reason, the conflict described in Scripture is not merely physical. It is the tension between a life directed by natural impulse and a life directed by the Spirit of God (Galatians 5:17).

When the soul follows its own reasoning, emotions, and desires apart from the guidance of the spirit, it aligns with the flesh. When it yields to what the spirit has received from God, it comes into alignment with the Spirit.

Throughout this chapter we will examine several experiences that illustrate how this conflict unfolds in everyday life. These moments reveal how fear can shape imagination, how emotional attachments can influence judgment, and how unseen spiritual realities can affect the inner life. Each example points to the same underlying truth: the soul must learn to align itself with the Spirit of God if it is to live in freedom and peace.

Understanding this battle prepares the believer for the teaching that follows. The conflict within the soul is real, but it is not without hope. God has provided truth, faith, and the guidance of the Holy Spirit so that the believer may stand firm in the midst of these struggles. As the soul learns to submit to the direction of the Spirit, the inner conflict that once produced confusion begins to give way to clarity and stability.

Managing the Imagination

Many people assume that if they truly had faith they would never experience internal struggle. Scripture, however, reveals that spiritual growth often involves learning how to deal with the conflict that arises within the soul.

The soul is the place where thoughts are formed, emotions are experienced, and choices are made. Because of this, it is also the place where fear, doubt, and imagination can attempt to challenge what the spirit has received from God.

The mind may begin to reason through circumstances and conclude that something God has promised is impossible. The emotions may react to external pressures with anxiety or discouragement. The imagination may create pictures of failure, danger or loss that feel more real than what God has spoken.

When these influences combine, the soul can become overwhelmed. The believer may know in the heart what God has said, yet still feel uncertainty in the mind and emotions. The spirit may hold firm to truth while the soul struggles to accept it.

This inner tension explains why Scripture repeatedly addresses the thoughts and imaginations of the mind.

The apostle Paul writes:

> *"Casting down imaginations, and every high thing that exalteth itself against the knowledge of God, and bringing into captivity every thought to the obedience of Christ."* (2 Corinthians 10:5)

This instruction shows that thoughts must be governed, not simply observed. It recognizes that thoughts and imaginations can rise within the soul in ways that challenge the truth that the spirit has received.

An imagination is not simply creative thinking. In this context it refers to mental constructions that oppose the knowledge and truth of God. These thoughts may arise from past experiences, fears, cultural assumptions, or external pressures. If they are not confronted, they can influence the decisions of the soul.

Confronting Fear Within the Soul

Among the most powerful influences within the soul is fear, which often plays a central role in this struggle. Fear is powerful because it works through the senses, amplifying what is seen and felt. What we see, hear, and experience in the natural world can create emotional reactions that feel overwhelming.

Circumstances may appear threatening. Situations may seem impossible to overcome. The soul may begin to react to these conditions with anxiety. Yet Scripture reminds us that fear does not originate from God, but it can take hold in the soul if left unchallenged.

Paul writes:

> *"For God hath not given us the spirit of fear; but of power, and of love, and of a sound mind."* (2 Timothy 1:7)

This verse reveals that fear often enters the life of a believer through external influences. What we see and hear in the world can stimulate fear in the mind and emotions of the soul. However, the spirit, or the hidden man of the heart, remains connected to the Spirit of God, who knows no fear. The challenge for the believer is learning how to respond when fear attempts to influence the soul.

At times, this conflict appears in simple but revealing ways. An experience from my own life illustrates this struggle. During a period when I was teaching a Bible study on freedom from fear, I encountered a situation that forced me to confront a long-standing fear of my own. I had inherited from my grandmother a deep fear of caterpillars. Snakes and other creatures did not trouble me, but caterpillars had always produced an intense reaction.

One day as I prepared to leave my rented home in Atlanta to visit a laundromat, I stepped outside and discovered that caterpillars covered the driveway, the yard, and even parts of the street. They had fallen from the pecan trees that hung over the house. Fear immediately rose within my soul.

I knew I had to leave the house, yet the sight of those creatures made even walking across the yard difficult. Gathering enough courage, I locked the doors and hurried to my car.

An hour later, I returned home, knowing I would have to face the same situation again. I imagined caterpillars falling on me as I stood at the door trying to unlock the house. The pictures in my mind seemed almost as real as the situation itself.

Inside the house, I paced back and forth, realizing something important. I could not teach others about freedom from fear if I was unwilling to confront fear in my own life. Eventually I picked up a broom and walked back outside to face the situation. To my amazement, the yard, driveway, and street were completely clear, not a single caterpillar remained.

As I stood there in surprise, the Holy Spirit spoke quietly within my heart: *"When you dealt with fear inside, I dealt with the caterpillars outside."*

That moment revealed something profound about the conflict within the soul. Fear had entered through my senses and taken hold in my imagination. The soul reacted emotionally to what it saw. However, once the fear inside was confronted and surrendered to God, the external situation changed in a way I could not have anticipated.

This experience reminded me that the greatest battles believers face are often not external but internal. What had appeared overwhelming externally had already been resolved internally. The battle was never about the caterpillars; it was about the condition of the soul.

The soul may react to circumstances with fear, doubt or confusion. Yet the spirit, connected to God, continues to call the soul to trust what God has spoken. Spiritual growth often involves learning how to bring the thoughts and emotions of the soul into alignment with the truth that the spirit has received. The believer learns to magnify the promises of God rather than the problems of circumstances.

This is why Scripture encourages believers to focus their attention on God rather than on the fears that arise from external conditions. The psalmist wrote:

> *"O magnify the Lord with me, and let us exalt his name together."* (Psalm 34:3)

To magnify something means to enlarge it in our vision. When we magnify problems, they appear overwhelming. When we magnify God, His power and faithfulness become greater in our perspective.

Gateways Into the Soul

To understand how these influences gain access, we must consider the gateways into the soul. Human experience enters the soul through gateways that God designed within the body. Among the most influential of these gateways are the eyes. What a person repeatedly looks at begins to shape the images formed within the mind and imagination, gradually shaping what the soul believes is real.

Scripture alludes to this influence when Jesus taught that the eye functions as the lamp of the body. When the eye is directed toward what is healthy and truthful, the inner life becomes filled with light. When the eye becomes fixed on things that distort or corrupt understanding, the soul gradually becomes affected by that influence. The images that enter through the eyes often become the thoughts and imaginations that later shape decisions.

For this reason, Scripture frequently connects vision with spiritual understanding. The apostle Paul prayed that the "eyes of the heart" would be enlightened so believers might perceive the hope and calling God has given them. This language suggests that perception occurs at more than one level. Physical sight allows us to see the world around us, yet spiritual understanding allows the inner person to see truth more clearly. When the soul becomes dominated by external images and impressions, confusion can arise. When the inner eyes are enlightened by the Spirit of God, the soul begins to perceive reality according to divine truth rather than according to the shifting impressions of circumstance.

Recognizing Spiritual Opposition

Scripture teaches that the struggle believers experience is not limited to visible circumstances. It is also influenced by external, unseen spiritual opposition. The apostle Paul explains that our battle is not ultimately against flesh and blood but against spiritual forces that oppose the purposes of God. These forces operate in an unseen realm yet influence human thinking, behavior, and societies in ways that often remain unnoticed. This explains why the battle for the soul can feel persistent and complex.

In describing this conflict, Paul identifies several forms of spiritual opposition. These are referred to as principalities, powers, rulers of the darkness of this world, and spiritual wickedness in high places (Ephesians 6:12). While the language may appear mysterious at first, it points to an organized resistance against the truth of God and the work of His kingdom.

Principalities can be understood as spiritual authorities that operate on a broad, systemic level of human life. Scripture suggests that these forces often operate in connection with cultural patterns, political systems, and societal attitudes that resist God's ways. Their influence can shape the moral direction of communities and even entire nations.

Powers represent spiritual influences that operate more directly within human experience. These forces work through deception, temptation, and confusion, seeking to distort the truth of God and lead people away from faith. They often target areas of personal weakness, attempting to draw individuals into patterns of thinking or behavior that separate them from God's purposes.

Paul also speaks of **rulers of the darkness** of this world. This expression emphasizes the way spiritual deception spreads through ideas and systems that obscure the light of truth. When false beliefs become widely accepted, entire cultures may begin to move in directions that contradict the character and wisdom of God.

Finally, Scripture refers to **spiritual wickedness in high places**. This phrase points to the elevation of influences that compete with God for devotion and trust. Anything that becomes an object of ultimate reliance – whether power, wealth, ideology or human authority – can function as an idol when it replaces dependence on God.

Understanding these realities helps believers interpret the struggles of life more clearly. The conflicts people experience are not always merely personal or social. Often, they reflect a deeper spiritual contest over truth, allegiance, and the direction of human life.

For this reason, Scripture calls believers to resist these influences not through hostility toward other people but through spiritual means. Truth, faith, righteousness, and the Word of God become the resources through which believers stand firm. The enemy may seek to deceive and divide, but the victory of Christ has already secured the ultimate outcome. Ultimately, these influences seek to shape the direction of the soul, but they do not have authority over a life submitted to God.

Recognizing the reality of spiritual opposition therefore leads not to fear but to vigilance. Believers are called to remain aware of the battle for the soul while trusting the authority and power of God to sustain them. Through obedience to Christ and reliance upon the Holy Spirit, the believer learns to stand steady in a world where unseen influences continually compete for the allegiance of the human heart.

The soul becomes the battlefield when it reacts to what it feels instead of responding to what the spirit has received from God. When the soul learns to trust the leadership of the spirit, inner peace begins to replace inner turmoil. The battle may continue, but it no longer defines the direction of life.

The soul gradually learns to follow the direction of the Spirit rather than reacting to the pressures of the moment, as it consistently yields to the direction of the spirit. Over time, the mind becomes steadier, the emotions become calmer, and the will becomes more confident in obeying God. The conflict within the soul does not disappear instantly, but it becomes easier to navigate as the believer grows in faith.

Yet another transformation still lies ahead. The soul must not only overcome conflict; it must also become **renewed and unified** so that thoughts, emotions, and decisions move together in harmony with the spirit.

In the next chapter, we will explore how the renewal of the mind brings the soul into greater unity, so that thoughts, emotions, and decisions begin to move together in alignment with the spirit.

Chapter 9

The Renewed Mind

If the soul is the place where thoughts, emotions, and decisions occur, then the transformation of the soul must begin with the **renewal of the mind**. Thus, the conflict described in the previous chapter finds its resolution here.

The mind serves as the primary gateway through which information enters the soul, and therefore, it plays a decisive role in directing the soul. What a person repeatedly thinks about eventually shapes how they feel and how they choose to act. Because of this, the condition of the mind has a powerful influence on the direction of life.

Scripture teaches that spiritual growth requires a change in the way a person thinks. The apostle Paul wrote:

> *"Be transformed by the renewing of your mind."*
> (Romans 12:2)

This transformation is not behavioral first. It is perceptual, changing how reality is interpreted. Essentially, transformation does not begin with outward behavior. It begins with a change in the inner life. When the mind is renewed, the soul gradually becomes aligned with the truth that the spirit has received from God. It becomes more responsive to the inward witness of the conscience, which reflects the voice of the spirit aligned with God.

Before this renewal occurs, the mind often operates according to patterns shaped by past experiences, cultural influences, and personal fears. These patterns may contradict the truth revealed in Scripture. As a result, the mind may question or resist what the spirit knows to be true.

The renewal of the mind occurs as a person is exposed to the Word of God and begins to meditate upon it regularly.

The psalmist described this process when he wrote:

> *"Blessed is the one… whose delight is in the law of the Lord, and who meditates on his law day and night." (Psalm 1:1–2)*

Meditation in this sense does not mean emptying the mind. It means filling the mind with the truth of God's Word and reflecting upon it until it becomes part of the believer's thinking, reshaping how the soul understands life.

As this process continues, the mind begins to adopt a new perspective. Thoughts that once seemed natural begin to change. Ideas that once dominated the soul lose their influence. Fear begins to give way to confidence in God. Doubt begins to give way to trust in His promises. Over time the mind learns to recognize the difference between thoughts that originate from human reasoning and those that align with the truth revealed by the Spirit of God.

This change in thinking produces stability within the soul. The emotions, which once reacted impulsively to circumstances, begin to settle under the influence of renewed thinking. Feelings are no longer the primary guide for decisions. Instead, the soul learns to respond according to the truth of God's Word.

The decision-making faculty of the soul, the will, also becomes strengthened through this renewal because clarity replaces confusion. Choices that once seemed difficult become clearer because the mind is now aligned with spiritual truth. Instead of constantly struggling between competing ideas, the soul begins to move in harmony with the spirit.

Scripture also encourages believers to actively guard what enters the mind. The eyes and ears serve as gateways through which information flows into the soul. What we see and hear influences the pictures formed in our imagination and the conclusions we draw about life. For this reason, believers are encouraged to focus their attention on things that strengthen faith rather than weaken it.

Paul advised believers to think about things that are true, honorable, and worthy of praise. When the mind dwells on these things, the soul becomes healthier and more stable.

Renewing the mind is therefore not a one-time event but a continual process. Each day the believer encounters new information, new experiences, and new challenges. The mind must continually return to the truth of God's Word in order to remain aligned with the spirit. As this process continues, something remarkable happens within the soul.

Thoughts, emotions, and decisions begin to move together in harmony. The mind no longer argues against what the spirit has received from God. The emotions no longer resist the path of obedience. The will no longer struggles to surrender control. Instead, the soul becomes unified. The mind understands the truth. The emotions support the truth. The will chooses to act upon the truth.

When this unity develops, the believer experiences a new level of spiritual stability. Life is no longer governed by fluctuating emotions or uncertain reasoning. Instead, the inner life is guided by the steady influence of God's Word. The spirit leads. The soul cooperates. The mind is renewed.

This renewal prepares the believer for the final stage of spiritual alignment. Once the spirit and soul are working together, the body becomes the instrument through which the inner life is expressed. To better understand this transformation, it is helpful to recognize that the mind can operate in different ways depending on what governs it.

The Three Expressions of the Mind

The Scriptures speak often about the mind, yet they do so in ways that reveal more than a single, simple function. The mind is not presented merely as a neutral processor of information. It reflects the condition of the inner life and can operate in different ways depending on what governs it. To understand the process of renewal, it is helpful to recognize three distinct expressions of the mind: the mind shaped by the soul, the mind aligned with the heart, and the mind of Christ.

These are not three separate minds existing independently within a person. Rather, they describe three ways in which the inner life can think, respond, and interpret reality.

The Mind Governed by the Soul

The mind governed by the soul reflects the natural tendencies of human thinking apart from the influence of God's Spirit. It is shaped by personal desire, emotional reaction, and self-preservation. This way of thinking often seeks control, resists correction, and leans toward its own understanding. This is the mind shaped by self rather than by truth.

Scripture describes this condition in strong terms. The apostle Paul explains that the mind set on the flesh is hostile toward God and does not submit to His law. This resistance does not always appear as open rebellion. It can also appear as subtle self-reliance, where the individual trusts personal reasoning above divine truth, which often feels reasonable but resists surrender.

The characteristics of this mindset can be seen in everyday life. It may express itself through fear, pride, defensiveness, or the desire to justify one's own position. It often avoids accountability, shifts blame when confronted, and seeks to protect itself at all costs. When challenged by truth, it may resist, reinterpret, or dismiss what it does not want to accept.

This way of thinking also affects speech and behavior. Jesus taught that what comes out of a person reveals what is within. Words that produce division, deception, or harm often originate from a mind that is not aligned with the truth of God. In this sense, the mind governed by the soul does not simply process information. It shapes the direction of life itself.

The Mind Aligned with the Heart

In contrast, the mind aligned with the heart reflects the influence of the hidden man of the heart, the inward person renewed by the Spirit of God. This mind is not driven by impulse or self-preservation but is oriented toward truth, humility, and obedience. This is the mind beginning to agree with what the spirit has received.

Scripture describes the inward man as incorruptible, marked by a meek and quiet spirit that is precious in the sight of God. This does not suggest weakness but rather a strength that rests in trust rather than control. The mind aligned with the heart listens before it speaks, receives before it reacts, and seeks understanding before forming conclusions because it is no longer driven by the need to defend itself.

This way of thinking develops as the believer grows in relationship with God. The Holy Spirit communicates truth to the inward man, and the mind begins to reflect that truth. Instead of being ruled by fear or pride, the mind becomes steady, attentive, and responsive to the direction of God.

The transformation of the mind does not occur instantly. It develops as the believer consistently turns toward the truth of God's Word. Over time, the patterns of thinking begin to change. What once produced anxiety may now produce trust. What once led to confusion may now lead to clarity. The mind becomes a place where the influence of the Spirit is increasingly evident.

The Mind of Christ

The highest expression of the renewed mind is described in Scripture as the mind of Christ, thinking shaped by the Spirit rather than by human limitation. The apostle Paul declares that believers have received not the spirit of the world but the Spirit who is from God, so that they may understand what God has freely given.

To have the mind of Christ does not mean possessing infinite knowledge or divine attributes in their fullness. Rather, it means sharing in the perspective, understanding, and priorities that come from the Spirit of

God. The believer begins to see life through the lens of God's truth rather than through the limitations of human reasoning alone.

This mind is formed through the work of the Holy Spirit. The Spirit reveals the things of God, guiding the believer into deeper understanding. Spiritual truth, which may appear unclear or even foolish from a purely natural perspective, becomes clear when discerned through the Spirit.

As this transformation takes place, the believer's thinking begins to reflect the character of Christ. Decisions are shaped by wisdom rather than impulse. Responses are guided by truth rather than emotion. The mind becomes increasingly aligned with the purposes of God.

The Renewal of the Mind

Understanding these expressions of the mind helps clarify the process of spiritual growth. The goal of the Christian life is not to eliminate thinking but to renew it, aligning thinking with truth. The mind that was once governed by the soul must come under the influence of the Spirit, so that it reflects the truth of God.

This renewal is an ongoing process. It requires intentional attention to what the mind receives, believes, and dwells upon. As the believer submits to the Word of God and responds to the leading of the Holy Spirit, the patterns of thinking begin to change.

The conflict described in Scripture often takes place at this very point. The soul may resist, while the Spirit leads. The old patterns may persist, while the new life calls for transformation. Yet through perseverance, truth begins to take root more deeply than habit or fear. In time, the mind becomes a place of alignment rather than conflict. The thoughts reflect truth, the responses reflect faith, and the life reflects the work of God within.

Spiritual Warfare in the Mind

Scripture teaches that believers live simultaneously in two dimensions of reality. We walk in physical bodies within the material world, yet our deepest conflicts are not ultimately physical. The apostle Paul explained this when he wrote that although we live in the flesh, we do not wage war according to the flesh. The struggles that shape human life often originate in a spiritual realm that cannot be seen with the natural eye. Thus, the renewal of the mind takes place in the context of spiritual conflict.

This reality becomes clearer when Paul describes the weapons available to believers. He explains that the weapons of our warfare are not carnal, meaning they are not merely human tools such as force, argument, or physical strength. Instead, they are spiritual in nature and are empowered by God for the purpose of tearing down strongholds. These strongholds are not physical structures but patterns of thought and belief that resist the truth of God.

For this reason, the battlefield of spiritual warfare is often located within the mind because this is where truth is either accepted or resisted. Paul describes this conflict in three related movements: *the pulling down of strongholds*, *the casting down of imaginations*, and *the bringing of thoughts into obedience to Christ*. Each phrase describes a different aspect of the transformation that takes place when the mind is renewed.

A stronghold may be understood as a deeply rooted belief or pattern of thinking that has become reinforced and firmly established over time. Such patterns can develop through personal experiences, cultural influences, or long-held assumptions about life. When these beliefs contradict the truth revealed in Scripture, they become barriers that resist spiritual understanding. The work of God's Word in the believer's life involves exposing those patterns and gradually replacing them with truth.

Paul also speaks of casting down imaginations and every high thing that exalts itself against the knowledge of God. Imagination, which we discussed in Chapter 8, here refers to the mental impressions and arguments that arise within the mind. These inner narratives can shape how people interpret their circumstances. Fear, doubt, resentment, and pride often begin as thoughts that appear reasonable at first but eventually grow into attitudes that oppose the knowledge of God.

The renewal of the mind involves learning to recognize these inner arguments and refusing to allow them to dominate the soul. Through prayer, meditation on Scripture, and obedience to the guidance of the Holy Spirit, believers gradually learn to measure their thoughts against the truth of God's Word. Thoughts that contradict that truth are not allowed to remain unchallenged but measured against God's truth.

The final step Paul describes is bringing every thought into captivity to the obedience of Christ so that the mind follows the spirit's direction rather than reacting to the pressures of the moment. This language suggests discipline and intentionality. The mind does not automatically remain aligned with truth. It must be guided, corrected, and sometimes restrained so that it follows the direction established by the spirit rather than the impulses of fear or pride.

When this process begins to take place, the believer's inner life gradually changes. Thoughts that once produced anxiety begin to give way to confidence in God's promises. Imaginations shaped by fear are replaced by expectations shaped by faith. The soul learns to follow the truth received by the spirit rather than reacting solely to the pressures of circumstance.

This is why the renewal of the mind is so central to spiritual maturity. The battle described in Scripture is not primarily fought through physical confrontation but through the transformation of the inner life. As the mind is renewed by truth, the strongholds that once resisted God begin to lose their power, and the soul becomes increasingly aligned with the purposes of Christ.

Remember, the battle that takes place within the mind did not begin in the mind itself. It is the result of a deeper disruption that occurred when humanity's direct communion with God was broken in the Garden of Eden (Genesis 3:8, 24). What was once a spirit-led existence became increasingly governed by the soul, as mankind began to rely on reasoning, emotion, and perception rather than the immediate guidance of God. So, basically, the fall of mankind shifted human life from spirit-led to soul-governed.

Through the work of Christ, access to God has been restored, as seen when the veil of the Temple was torn (Matthew 27:51). Yet the effects of that original shift remain evident in the inner life. The mind has become a primary battleground where the soul must be brought back into alignment with the spirit. Spiritual warfare, therefore, is not only external opposition but the ongoing renewal of the inner man, representing the restoration of proper order within the inner life.

Spiritual warfare, at its core, is about learning to love God with the mind. To love God with the soul includes the renewal of thought. The mind must be trained to agree with the will and Word of God rather than the patterns of fear, doubt, or imagination that arise from the world. As Scripture teaches, we are transformed by the renewing of our minds (Romans 12:2). In this way, loving God is not passive. It involves actively choosing truth over deception and aligning our thoughts, reasoning, and imagination with what God has spoken.

The Foundation of Truth

In Paul's description of the armor of God, the first element mentioned is the girdle, or belt, of truth. In the armor of a Roman soldier, the belt served a crucial purpose. It gathered the other pieces of armor together and allowed the soldier to move freely and effectively in battle. Without the belt securing the armor, the soldier's movements would become hindered and the rest of the equipment would not function properly. Paul uses this image to illustrate the foundational role truth plays in the spiritual life of the believer.

Truth provides the structure that holds the entire inner life together. When a person's understanding is anchored in truth, the mind becomes stable and the soul gains clarity about what is real and trustworthy. Without that foundation, the mind becomes vulnerable to confusion, deception, and shifting opinions. The renewal of the mind therefore begins with recognizing that truth is not merely an abstract idea but a reality rooted in the nature and character of God Himself.

Scripture repeatedly emphasizes that truth originates with God. Jesus declared that God is spirit and that those who worship Him must worship in spirit and in truth. In another passage He identified Himself as the way, the truth, and the life. These statements reveal that truth is not simply information or philosophy. Truth is the character and revelation of God made known through Christ. When the believer embraces this truth, the inner life becomes anchored in something greater than personal feelings or cultural assumptions.

Because truth reflects the character of God, it also shapes the conduct of those who follow Him. The apostle John warned that denying the identity of Christ is the essence of deception. In contrast, acknowledging the Son reveals a heart aligned with the Father. Scripture further reminds us that God does not lie or change His mind as we sometimes do. His promises remain reliable, and His word provides a firm foundation for faith.

Truth also governs the believer's relationships with others. The apostle Paul instructed the church to put away falsehood and to speak truth with one another because believers belong to the same spiritual body. Honesty preserves unity, while deception fractures trust within the community. Proverbs 12:19 echoes this principle by declaring that truthful lips endure, while lies are temporary and destructive.

Finally, truth requires honesty within the individual soul. The Scriptures warn that if a person claims to be without sin, they deceive themselves and the truth is not present within them. Spiritual maturity therefore involves the willingness to examine one's own life honestly before God. The girdle of truth is not merely a doctrinal position but a posture of sincerity before the Lord.

When truth secures the inner life in this way, the other elements of spiritual defense begin to function properly. The mind becomes able to discern error, the soul learns to resist deception, and the believer stands firmly upon the promises of God. Truth therefore forms the first and most essential element in the armor of God, because every other spiritual weapon depends upon it.

The Assurance That Guards the Mind

In Paul's description of the armor of God, believers are instructed to take the helmet of salvation. In ancient warfare the helmet protected the head, the most vulnerable and essential part of the soldier's body. A blow to the head could end a battle instantly. Paul uses this image to illustrate the importance of guarding the mind in the believer's spiritual life.

Salvation provides that protection. Through the grace of God, believers are brought into a restored relationship with Him, not through human effort but through the work of Christ. Scripture teaches that it is by grace that we have been saved through faith, and that this salvation is the gift of God rather than the result of human achievement. Because salvation originates with God, it establishes a secure foundation for the believer's identity and hope.

This assurance plays an important role in the renewal of the mind. Many of the struggles believers face arise when doubts about God's acceptance begin to trouble the soul. Thoughts of failure, guilt, or inadequacy can gradually weaken a person's confidence before God. The helmet of salvation protects the mind from these influences by anchoring identity in God's grace rather than human performance.

Scripture also encourages believers to continue growing in the reality of their salvation. The apostle Paul wrote to the Philippians that they should work out their salvation with reverence and humility, recognizing that God Himself is at work within them. This instruction does not mean that salvation must be earned. Instead, it means that the life given through Christ continues to unfold as believers respond to the work of the Holy Spirit within them.

In this way salvation becomes both a gift and a continuing transformation. God places within the believer both the desire and the ability to pursue what pleases Him. As the mind becomes increasingly aware of this truth, confidence replaces uncertainty and hope replaces fear because the foundation no longer depends on self. The helmet of salvation therefore protects the believer not only from external opposition but also from the internal doubts that can arise within the soul.

When the assurance of salvation guards the mind, the believer is able to face spiritual conflict with stability. Accusations, discouragement, and fear may still appear, yet they do not determine the outcome. The mind remains anchored in the knowledge that God has begun a work that He intends to complete.

For this reason, the helmet of salvation forms an essential part of the believer's spiritual armor. It protects the mind, preserves confidence in God's grace, and allows the soul to remain steady while the rest of the battle unfolds.

Transforming the Mind

When people begin to believe lies about God, themselves or others, those false beliefs can shape behavior and culture in destructive ways. Thus, believers are instructed to remain aware that the ultimate enemy is not another person but the deception that influences the mind.

Recognizing this distinction changes how believers respond to conflict. Instead of viewing other people as enemies, believers learn to address the deeper spiritual influences at work. Prayer, truth, faith, and obedience become the means by which believers resist deception and remain aligned with God's purposes. The renewal of the mind is the process by which the soul learns to agree with what the truth that spirit has received from God. Renewing the mind is not a one-time event, but a continuous practice of shifting how you interpret life's continual challenges. The Bible states in 2 Corinthians 10:5 to "take every thought captive to make it obedient to Christ."

This perspective also protects the believer from becoming overwhelmed by fear, negativity, and shame. Scripture consistently affirms that these spiritual forces do not operate outside the authority of God. The victory of Christ over sin and death establishes the foundation upon which believers stand. Through the work of Christ and the guidance of the Holy Spirit, the believer is equipped to resist deception and remain faithful to the truth.

The armor of God is not a symbol of fear but of confidence. Each piece of spiritual armor represents a resource God has given so that believers can remain steady in the midst of opposition. Truth stabilizes the mind, righteousness guards the heart, faith protects the soul, and the Word of God confronts deception directly.

Understanding the reality of spiritual opposition therefore leads not to anxiety but to greater dependence upon God. When believers recognize where the true conflict lies, they are able to respond with wisdom rather than confusion. The battle may be unseen, but the resources God provides are more than sufficient for those who trust Him. As the mind is renewed, the soul becomes stable, and the life begins to reflect the order God intended from the beginning.

In the next chapter we will explore what happens when the soul becomes fully aligned with the spirit and how this unity prepares the believer to live a life that reflects God's purposes in the world.

Chapter 10

The Unified Soul

The spiritual life begins in the heart, the hidden man within. From that inner place, the Spirit of God communicates truth, direction, and purpose. Yet the transformation of a person does not stop with the heart alone. What begins in the heart must now become fully aligned within the soul, meaning the soul must also come into harmony with what the spirit has received. When this harmony develops, the soul becomes unified, resolving the conflict described in earlier chapters.

A unified soul is one in which the mind, emotions, and will work together rather than against one another. The mind understands the truth of God's Word. The emotions support that truth instead of resisting it. The will chooses to act in obedience to what the spirit has received rather than competing for control. In this state, the inner conflict that once troubled the soul begins to fade.

Earlier we saw how the soul can become divided. The mind may question what the spirit believes. Emotions may respond with fear or discouragement. The will may hesitate to act even when the heart knows what is right. However, as the mind is renewed through the Word of God and the soul learns to trust the leadership of the spirit, these divisions gradually diminish. The inner life becomes more stable.

Instead of reacting impulsively to circumstances, the soul begins to respond according to spiritual truth. The mind remembers what God has said. The emotions begin to align with that confidence. The will chooses obedience even when circumstances appear uncertain. This unity creates a remarkable sense of inner peace.

The believer is no longer pulled in multiple directions by conflicting thoughts and feelings. Instead, there is clarity about what God desires and confidence in following that direction.

This inner alignment reflects the design God intended for human life. The spirit receives guidance from God. The soul agrees with that guidance. The body carries out the resulting action. When the soul is unified in this way, the believer begins to live from the inside out.

Scripture encourages believers to pursue this kind of inner harmony. When the psalmist speaks about meditating on the Word of God day and night, he is describing a process through which the soul gradually becomes aligned with divine truth. The mind learns to think according to God's wisdom.

As the mind changes, the emotions also become more stable. Fear gives way to confidence as truth becomes more authoritative than experience. Anxiety gives way to peace as confidence anchors uncertainty. The emotional life becomes less controlled by circumstances and more influenced by trust in God. The will also becomes stronger and more decisive. Rather than wavering between competing desires, the soul learns to choose the path that aligns with the spirit.

This unity does not mean that challenges disappear. Life continues to present difficulties, pressures, and uncertainties. However, the believer approaches those situations with a different inner posture. Instead of being controlled by external circumstances, the soul remains anchored in the truth received by the spirit.

The believer begins to experience the stability described in Scripture as a sound mind. This soundness of mind reflects an inner order that develops when the spirit and soul are working together. Thoughts are clearer. Emotions are steadier. Decisions are guided by wisdom rather than impulse.

As this alignment strengthens, the believer becomes increasingly capable of living in obedience to God even in difficult situations. The unified soul also prepares the believer for the outward expression of spiritual life. Yet alignment alone does not fully account for the condition of the soul. The soul must not only be brought into order, but it must also be restored.

The Cleansing of the Soul

A unified soul is not achieved through discipline alone. Alignment of the mind, emotions, and will requires more than effort. It requires cleansing. The soul must not only be brought into order, but also restored from the effects of sin, memory, and internal fragmentation.

Throughout Scripture, the condition of the soul is never treated as neutral. It is shaped by what it has received, what it has believed, and what it has carried. Even after coming to God, many continue to struggle within because the soul still bears the imprint of past wounds, false beliefs, and unresolved patterns. Unity within the soul, therefore, is not simply the result of right thinking. It is the result of divine intervention.

This is where the work of Christ becomes central. The same power that restores the spirit to God also provides cleansing for the soul. What cannot be undone through reasoning or emotional effort is addressed through the redemptive work of Jesus. The soul is not merely instructed into alignment. It is washed, renewed, and restored.

The Blood That Cleanses and Restores

The restoration of the soul is rooted in the finished work of Christ, who sacrificed His life. Scripture teaches that "the life of the flesh is in the blood" and that it is the blood that makes atonement for the soul (Leviticus 17:11). From the beginning, God established that sin could not be addressed apart from sacrifice. Life would have to be given in exchange for life. This principle reaches its fulfillment in Jesus Christ, whose blood was not merely shed as an act of suffering, but offered as the final and perfect sacrifice to redeem humanity and restore fellowship with God.

To understand the depth of this truth, one must move beyond intellectual agreement into spiritual perception. The work of Christ is not fully grasped by observation alone. It must be received by faith, seen through the Word, and embraced within the heart. The believer is invited to behold, not with natural eyes, but with spiritual understanding, the fullness of what His blood has accomplished.

The story begins with a birth unlike any other. Jesus was conceived not by the will or bloodline of man, but by the Holy Spirit (Matthew 1:18; Luke 1:35). His blood was therefore untainted by the fallen nature of humanity. He entered the world as both fully man and fully God, uniquely qualified to stand as a spotless sacrifice.

This pattern of redemption was foreshadowed in the book of Exodus when the blood of the lamb was placed upon the doorposts of the homes of Israel (Exodus 12:7, 13). When the death angel passed through the land, the blood became the distinguishing mark of protection. Death could not enter where the blood had been applied. This was not merely symbolic but spiritually effective. It was a declaration that life would be preserved where substitution had been made.

The suffering of Christ further reveals the cost of redemption. The prophet Isaiah declares that "by his stripes we are healed" (Isaiah 53:5), pointing to the physical wounds He endured. The crown of thorns pressed into His head (Matthew 27:29; John 19:2–5) and the piercing of His side (John 19:34) testify to the completeness of His sacrifice. His blood was not shed in part but fully given.

Jesus Himself spoke of this reality in a way that challenged those who heard Him, declaring that one must eat His flesh and drink His blood (John 6:53–56). This was not an invitation to physical consumption, but to spiritual participation. In Communion, the believer partakes of the bread and cup in remembrance of Him (Luke 22:19–20), entering into a living awareness of His sacrifice. It is a moment where faith engages what the senses cannot fully perceive.

The imagery reaches its fulfillment in the heavenly reality described in Hebrews, where Christ is seen as the High Priest who entered the true Holy Place and presented His own blood for our atonement (Hebrews 9:11–12). What was once performed yearly under the old covenant has now been accomplished once and for all.

The work of Christ does not merely cleanse the soul in a general sense. Scripture reveals that the blood of Jesus accomplishes several distinct and powerful realities in the life of the believer. Through His blood, we are redeemed, delivered from the power of sin and brought into right relationship with God (Ephesians 1:7; 1 Peter 1:18–19). What was once held in bondage is now purchased and restored.

Beyond cleansing and redemption, the believer is justified. "Having now been justified by His blood, we shall be saved from wrath through Him" (Romans 5:9). Justification means that the soul no longer stands condemned but is declared righteous before God. We were made righteous, or *just-as-if-ied* never sinned. Thus, we have been deemed not guilty, saved from the wrath of God.

The blood also sanctifies, setting the believer apart for God's purposes (Hebrews 13:12). What once belonged to the world is now marked as belonging to God. The root *sanct-* signifies holiness, meaning sanctification is the process of becoming a "saint" (set apart) in daily life. Unlike justification, sanctification is a lifelong journey of "putting off" sin and "putting on" Christ-like character, guided by the Holy Spirit.

In addition, the life of God flows through the blood, and through Christ, that life becomes the source of spiritual vitality within the believer. Scripture further reveals that the blood speaks on our behalf. It intercedes, declaring mercy rather than judgment (Hebrews 12:24). Even when words fail, the finished work of Christ continues to speak. Finally, the blood grants access. "We have confidence to enter the Most Holy Place by the blood of Jesus" (Hebrews 10:19). What was once separated is now open. The barrier has been removed.

When these truths are received together, the believer begins to understand that the blood of Jesus does more than forgive sin. It cleanses, restores, protects, and reconciles the condition of the soul itself. It opens access to God, not through human effort, but through divine provision. The soul, once stained and separated, is now made clean and brought back into unity with God.

Healing and Restoration of the Soul

The unification of the soul is not achieved through discipline alone. It is the result of restoration. The mind, emotions, and will do not come into alignment simply by effort, but by the healing work of God within the inner life. Scripture reveals that this healing was accomplished through the finished work of Christ. The prophet Isaiah declared, *"He was wounded for our transgressions, he was bruised for our iniquities... and with his stripes we are healed"* (Isaiah 53:5). This healing is not limited to the physical body. It extends to the entire person: spirit, soul, and body.

The apostle Peter confirms this truth, writing, *"Who his own self bare our sins in his own body on the tree... by whose stripes ye were healed"* (1 Peter 2:24). Through the sacrifice of Jesus, provision has been made not only for forgiveness, but for restoration. The soul, once fragmented by sin, fear, and disorder, can be made whole.

This restoration is closely connected to the renewal of the mind. As Paul writes in the book of Romans, *"Be transformed by the renewing of your mind"* (Romans 12:2). The mind must be retrained to think in alignment with truth. Old patterns of fear, doubt, and self-reliance are replaced with confidence in the Word of God. As the mind is renewed, the emotions begin to stabilize, and the will becomes increasingly surrendered to God.

Healing within the soul is therefore both a gift and a process. It is a gift because it has already been provided through Christ. It is a process because it must be received, believed, and lived out over time. So, it is already accomplished, yet progressively experienced.

As this work continues, alignment begins to take place. The spirit, connected to God, provides direction. The renewed mind interprets that direction correctly. The emotions come into agreement rather than resistance. The will chooses obedience rather than independence. What was once divided becomes unified, as truth replaces distortion and trust replaces fear.

This is the picture of a restored soul. The believer no longer lives in internal conflict but in inward harmony. Thought, feeling, and decision begin to move together under the influence of the Spirit of God. The result is not perfection, but stability. Neither is there the absence of challenge, but the presence of order. The unified soul is, therefore, not merely disciplined; it is healed, renewed, and aligned with God, responding consistently to the direction of the spirit.

Bodily Expression

Up to this point we have focused primarily on the inward dimensions of human existence: the spirit and the soul. However, God did not design spiritual life to remain hidden within a person. It was always meant to be expressed. What begins in the heart and is stabilized within the soul must eventually be expressed through the body.

As established previously, the heart is the inward center of life, the hidden man is the person within that center, and the spirit is the deepest part of that person through which God is known. This means that when God speaks, He does not speak to the outer person first or the mind alone.

He speaks to the inward man, specifically to the spirit, where understanding is received before it is processed. From that place, what is received must pass through the soul, where it is interpreted, accepted, or resisted. Finally, it is expressed through the body in word and action. From reception to expression, this is the full movement of spiritual life.

The body becomes the instrument revealing what has taken place within. Words spoken, actions taken, and relationships formed all reflect the condition of the heart and the alignment of the soul. When the spirit is connected to God and the soul is unified under that leadership, the body becomes a powerful instrument for expressing the purposes of God in the world.

In the next part of this book, we will explore how the life of the spirit and soul becomes visible through the body and how believers learn to live their daily lives as expressions of the spiritual transformation that has taken place within. When the heart believes, the soul aligns, and the body obeys, the command of Christ is fulfilled, and believers begin to love God with their whole being.

PART III – THE BODY

Living the Spiritual Life

Chapter 11

The Body as the Temple

Up to this point we have explored the inward dimensions of human life. The heart, the hidden man within, receives truth from God. The soul processes that truth through thought, emotion, and decision. When the spirit and soul become aligned, the believer begins to experience stability and clarity within the inner life. However, the spiritual life does not remain hidden inside a person. What begins within must eventually be expressed outwardly. This outward expression occurs through the body. Otherwise, it remains incomplete.

The body is the visible dimension of human life. Through the body we interact with the world around us. We speak, act, work, move, and relate to others through physical presence. Because of this, the body becomes the instrument through which thc condition of the inner life is revealed.

Scripture places great importance on the role of the body in spiritual life. The apostle Paul reminds believers that the body is not merely a physical structure but a sacred dwelling place.

> *"Do you not know that your bodies are temples of the Holy Spirit, who is in you, whom you have received from God?"* (1 Corinthians 6:19)

A temple is a place where God's presence dwells. In the Old Testament the temple was a physical building where people gathered to worship and where the presence of God was revealed in a special way. In the New Testament, however, God no longer dwells in buildings made by human hands. Instead, He chooses to dwell within His people.

The body therefore becomes a temple, a living place where the Spirit of God resides spiritually, not symbolically. This truth changes the way believers understand the physical dimension of life. The body is not simply a tool for survival or personal enjoyment. It is an instrument through which the presence and purposes of God can be expressed.

Because the body serves this sacred role, Scripture teaches that what is done in the body matters. The apostle Paul wrote that each person will one day give account for the things done while living in the body (2 Corinthians 5:10). This reminder emphasizes that physical actions carry spiritual significance. Words spoken, deeds performed, and habits practiced all reflect the condition of the inner life. The body, therefore, reveals what the heart and soul truly believe.

If the spirit is aligned with God and the soul is unified under that leadership, the body begins to express that alignment through actions that reflect obedience and love. Words become more careful. Behavior becomes more disciplined. Relationships begin to reflect the character of Christ. However, when the soul resists the leadership of the spirit, the body may express confusion, anger or selfishness.

In this way, the body serves as a mirror of the inner life, revealing the condition of the soul and the direction of the spirit. Jesus illustrated this principle when He taught that a tree is known by its fruit. The fruit does not create the tree; it reveals it. A healthy tree produces good fruit, while a corrupted tree produces fruit that reflects its condition. The same is true of human life. The actions of the body reveal the condition of the heart.

This does not mean believers become perfect in their outward behavior. Spiritual growth remains a lifelong journey. Yet as the spirit leads and the soul cooperates, the body increasingly becomes an instrument of righteousness rather than an instrument of confusion.

Scripture encourages believers to present their bodies to God in service to His purposes. Instead of allowing the body to be governed by impulse or selfish desire, the believer learns to use physical actions as expressions of devotion to God. Hands become instruments of service. Feet carry the believer into places where help and encouragement are needed. The voice becomes a tool for speaking truth and encouragement. Even ordinary actions take on spiritual significance when they flow from a heart aligned with God.

The body also serves another important purpose. It allows the inward work of God to become visible to others. Faith that remains hidden within the heart cannot easily be seen. However, when faith expresses itself through actions, such as kindness, generosity, patience, and integrity, others begin to witness the reality of God's work within a person.

The body becomes the means through which spiritual life touches the world. It is the means through which love for God and others is expressed. This is why Scripture encourages believers to live in a way that reflects the character of Christ. The transformation that begins in the spirit and is stabilized in the soul must eventually be demonstrated in daily life.

To love God with the body is to present it as "a living sacrifice, holy, acceptable to God" (Romans 12:1). Every action, every word, and every choice becomes an opportunity to reflect what has taken place within.

What begins in the heart and is formed within the soul is ultimately revealed through the body. In this way, love for God becomes visible. It is no longer confined to belief or intention but is demonstrated through a life of obedience, worship, and surrender.

Guarding the Heart With Righteousness

In Paul's description of the armor of God, the breastplate represents righteousness. In the armor worn by ancient soldiers, the breastplate protected the chest and the vital organs beneath it. Without this protection, the soldier's most vulnerable areas would be exposed to attack. Paul draws upon this image to explain how righteousness protects the inner life of the believer.

The Scriptures frequently describe the heart as the center of human life. It is the place where belief forms, where decisions take root, and where the direction of life is ultimately determined. Because the heart holds such influence over a person's life, it must be guarded carefully. Proverbs expresses this idea clearly when it says, "Keep thy heart with all diligence; for out of it are the issues of life." What occupies the heart eventually shapes the words a person speaks and the actions they choose.

Righteousness provides the protection that guards this inner life. The believer's righteousness does not originate in personal moral perfection but in the redemptive work of Jesus Christ. Through His sacrifice, Christ took upon Himself the burden of human sin so that those who trust in Him might be brought into right standing with God. Scripture describes this transformation by saying that Christ "was made to be sin for us... that we might be made the righteousness of God in Him."

This truth changes how believers understand their relationship with God. Rather than living in constant awareness of failure, the follower of Christ learns to live with the confidence that reconciliation with God has been accomplished through Christ. The righteousness given through Christ establishes a new identity. It allows the believer to approach God not as one permanently condemned but as one restored to fellowship.

At the same time, this righteousness shapes the way life is lived. When the heart is protected by righteousness, the believer becomes increasingly attentive to the character of God. The words of Scripture are stored within the heart so that they guide decisions and guard against temptation. As the psalmist declared, "Thy word have I hid in mine heart, that I might not sin against thee." The presence of God's truth within the heart becomes a protective influence that strengthens the soul against corruption. It ensures the soul remains aligned and the body responds rightly.

The breastplate of righteousness, therefore, represents both a gift and a responsibility received through Christ, expressed through life. It reminds believers that their standing before God has been secured through Christ, and it also calls them to live in a way that reflects that new identity. When the heart remains guarded by righteousness, the inward life becomes stable, and the outward life begins to reflect the character of the One who has redeemed it.

Instrument of Obedience

The world may not be able to see the hidden man of the heart, but it can see the actions of the body. When the body becomes an instrument of obedience, the invisible work of God becomes visible through the lives of His people.

Yet among all the ways the body expresses the inner life, there is one that gathers every action, word, and intention into a single offering. In the next chapter, we will explore worship as the highest expression of the body, where the life formed within is consciously and fully directed toward God.

Chapter 12

The Body in Worship

Worship is often thought of as an inward experience that takes place primarily within the heart or mind. Many people imagine worship as a quiet spiritual feeling expressed through thought, reflection, or prayer. While the inner life certainly plays an essential role in worship, Scripture presents a broader picture. Biblical worship involves the whole person – spirit, soul, and body – working together in reverence toward God in unity.

Human beings were created as integrated creatures designed to function as one unified life. The spirit communes with God, the soul thinks and feels, and the body expresses outwardly what the inner life believes. When these dimensions operate in harmony, worship becomes more than a mental exercise. It becomes the outward expression of an inward relationship with the Creator.

The apostle Paul describes this connection clearly when he writes, "Present your bodies a living sacrifice, holy and acceptable unto God, which is your reasonable service." This instruction reveals that worship is not confined to words spoken in prayer or songs sung in church. Worship includes the way the body itself is offered to God in obedience and devotion.

The body therefore becomes more than a biological structure that allows us to move through the physical world. It becomes an instrument through which the inner life expresses honor toward God as a response to what He has already done within. When the spirit and soul are aligned with the Lord, the body participates in that devotion through posture, action, and obedience.

Worship, in its fullest sense, involves the whole person responding to God with reverence, gratitude, and surrender, not to earn His favor, but to reflect it.

The Body in Praise and Reverence

Scripture repeatedly shows that worship involves physical expression. Throughout the Bible people bow, kneel, lift their hands, sing, and even fall on their faces before God. These actions are not empty rituals. They represent outward signs of inward devotion and reverence.

The psalmist invites the people of God with these words: "O come, let us worship and bow down: let us kneel before the Lord our maker." The posture of the body reflects the posture of the heart. Bowing acknowledges the authority of God. Kneeling expresses humility before His greatness. Lifting the hands symbolizes surrender and praise.

These physical expressions remind believers that worship is not merely intellectual agreement with religious ideas. Worship is a response of the entire person to the presence and character of God. The body participates in that response because the body is part of the person God created.

When the body expresses reverence, the soul often follows more deeply into the experience of worship. The physical act of kneeling may quiet the mind and focus the attention of the soul. Raising the hands in praise may lift the heart toward gratitude. In this way, the body and soul cooperate in directing attention toward God.

This relationship also explains why Scripture encourages believers to use their bodies in acts of devotion. Singing praises, lifting the voice in prayer, and serving others through physical action are all forms of worship. The body becomes the visible expression of the faith that resides within the hidden man of the heart.

True worship, therefore, moves from the inside outward. The spirit recognizes the greatness of God, the soul responds with gratitude and reverence, and the body expresses that devotion through action.

The Embodied Savior

The importance of the body in worship becomes even clearer when we consider the life of Jesus Christ. Christianity is not a disembodied spirituality removed from physical reality. The central confession of the faith declares that *the Word became flesh and dwelt among us* (John 1:14).

The Son of God entered human history through a physical body. He walked the roads of Galilee, touched the sick, embraced children, and endured suffering on the cross. His incarnation reveals that God does not reject the physical dimension of human life. Instead, He entered it fully in order to redeem it.

Because Christ came in the flesh, the body becomes a meaningful part of the believer's relationship with God. Worship is not an escape from the physical world but a transformation of how the physical life is lived. The same body that once served selfish desires can now become an instrument dedicated to the service of God.

The resurrection of Jesus reinforces this truth. Christ did not rise as a disembodied spirit. He rose with a glorified body, demonstrating that redemption extends to the whole person. The future hope of believers includes not only spiritual renewal but the restoration of the body as well. Understanding this truth changes how we view worship. The body is not an obstacle to spiritual life. It is a vessel through which spiritual life can be expressed.

The Body in Remembrance: Communion

One of the clearest ways the body participates in worship is through the act of communion. In this sacred moment, the believer does not merely think about Christ's sacrifice but engages in a physical act that reflects a spiritual reality. Bread is taken, a cup is received, and through these simple elements, the believer is called to remember the broken body and shed blood of Jesus Christ.

On one occasion during a Wednesday evening Bible class at the Cathedral at Chapel Hill, Archbishop Earl Paulk introduced the concept of *transubstantiation*. He explained that, according to this teaching, although the bread and wine appear unchanged, they are understood to become the body and blood of Christ. That statement stirred something deeply within me. As a teacher and visual learner, I wanted to understand more fully what this meant.

Later, at home, I placed a communion cup in front of me and reflected on what had been shared. As I focused on the elements, something unexpected occurred. Suddenly, what seemed to be a cloud began to form and slowly move into the room from the right side of my office. It approached me as I stood before the blackboard and the communion cup, and I became aware that I was experiencing an open vision (Chapter 7).

As the cloud drew nearer, I sensed the presence of Jesus within it. It stopped directly in front of me, filling the space. Though the physical elements in front of me remained unchanged, something deeper was taking place. In that moment, I understood that what I was seeing was not about physical transformation, but spiritual reality. The bread and the cup, though outwardly the same, were no longer ordinary to me. Jesus was present.

The awareness of His presence overwhelmed me. I began to weep, followed by a deep sense of joy. What I experienced was more than a moment of reflection. It was a personal encounter that confirmed what I had begun to understand. Communion was not merely symbolic. It was a point of real spiritual participation.

What I encountered was not a change in the elements themselves, but a deeper awareness of the spiritual reality they represent. Jesus did not say that the bread represents His body or that the cup represents His blood. He said, "This is my body... this is my blood" (Luke 22:19–20). These words invite the believer to move beyond outward appearance and to recognize a deeper reality that is received by faith.

Communion is therefore not simply an act of remembrance in the intellectual sense. It is an act of participation. When the believer receives the bread and the cup, the body is engaged in a moment that reflects a spiritual truth. The hands receive, the mouth partakes, and the heart responds. Worship, in this sense, involves the whole person.

The apostle Paul warns that this act must not be taken lightly. In the book of 1 Corinthians, he writes that those who partake "in an unworthy manner" fail to discern the Lord's body and may bring judgment upon themselves (1 Corinthians 11:27–30). This warning does not discourage participation but calls for reverence. Communion is not casual. It is sacred.

When approached with understanding, communion becomes a powerful moment of alignment. The believer remembers the sacrifice of Christ, reflects on the meaning of His broken body and shed blood, and renews commitment to live in accordance with that sacrifice. It is a moment where the inward reality of faith is expressed through outward action.

To truly grasp the depth of this moment is to recognize what took place at the cross. The body of Jesus was broken, bearing the weight of sin. His blood was shed, providing cleansing and access to God. As the prophet Isaiah declares, "by his wounds we are healed" (Isaiah 53:5). This is not merely a historical event to recall, but a reality to receive.

When the believer participates in communion with understanding, something shifts. Thanksgiving rises. Worship deepens. The awareness of Christ's presence becomes more real. The act itself becomes a doorway into deeper fellowship with God. No one truly encounters the presence of Christ and remains unchanged.

Communion engages the body in a way that draws the entire person into remembrance, reverence, and renewed alignment. This is why Jesus instructed His followers to continue this practice. It is not for His sake, but for ours. Each time communion is received, the believer is reminded of who Christ is, what He has done, and what has been made available through Him. The body participates in that remembrance, and through that participation, the entire person is drawn into worship.

Worship Through Daily Life

Worship is sometimes associated primarily with gatherings of believers in churches or places of prayer. These gatherings are important and valuable, yet Scripture presents worship as something that extends far beyond a single location or moment in time, into every moment of daily life

Paul's instruction to present the body as a living sacrifice suggests that worship continues throughout the daily activities of life. The way a person works, speaks, serves, and treats others can all become expressions of devotion to God.

When the believer offers daily actions to the Lord with intention, ordinary moments become acts of worship. Serving a neighbor, speaking words that bring encouragement, and performing work with integrity all reflect a life offered to God. The body becomes the instrument through which the love of God touches the world.

This understanding broadens the meaning of worship. Worship is not limited to music or formal prayer. Worship is the life of a believer lived in obedience and gratitude toward God.

Such worship requires attentiveness to the condition of the inner life. When the spirit remains connected to God and the soul remains aligned with His truth, the body naturally becomes an instrument of righteousness.

Worship and Alignment

The relationship between spirit, soul, and body becomes especially important when considering the nature of worship. True worship flows from a heart that recognizes God's authority and goodness. When the hidden man of the heart is aligned with God, the soul begins to reflect that alignment through thought, emotion, and decision.

Once the spirit and soul move together in harmony, the body expresses what the inner life has embraced. Words spoken in praise, actions performed in obedience, and service offered to others become visible expressions of inward devotion.

When the inner life is divided, worship can become mechanical or empty. A person may sing words of praise while the mind remains distracted or the heart remains distant from God. Scripture consistently calls believers to avoid this kind of divided devotion (1 Corinthians 7:35), which occurs when the body acts without inward agreement.

God desires worship that flows from sincerity. When the heart, soul, and body move together in unity, worship becomes authentic and powerful. The whole person responds to God with reverence and gratitude in unity rather than division. This alignment reflects the design God established for human life from the beginning.

The Body as a Visible Witness

When the body is offered to God in worship, it becomes more than a personal expression of devotion. It also becomes a witness to others. The way a believer lives, serves, and conducts daily life communicates something about the reality of God. Acts of kindness, patience, and integrity, for instance, reveal the influence of the Spirit within the believer. Even small actions performed with love can become visible signs of God's presence in the world. In this way, the body becomes a testimony. The inward transformation brought by God begins to appear in outward conduct. Others may see the peace, humility, and compassion expressed through the believer's life and become curious about the source of that transformation. Worship, therefore, carries both personal and communal significance. The believer honors God through obedience while simultaneously reflecting God's character to the world.

Living Worship

When worship is understood in this way, the believer begins to see life itself as an opportunity to honor God. Every action of the body can become an expression of devotion when it is guided by a heart aligned with the Spirit. The spirit receives guidance from God. The soul responds with faith and understanding. The body expresses that devotion through speech, action, and service.

This pattern reflects the design God placed within human life. The inward man leads, the soul cooperates, and the body responds consistently, becoming the visible instrument of obedience. In this way, worship becomes a way of living rather than a momentary activity. Believers learn to walk through daily life aware that every action can honor the One who created and redeemed them. The body, once merely an instrument of physical existence, becomes a vessel through which the life of God is expressed in the world.

Among all the ways the body expresses the inner life, one stands out above the rest. The **tongue**, the instrument of speech, has extraordinary power to reveal what resides within the heart.

In the next chapter we will examine how speech becomes the bridge between the inner life and the outward world, and why the words spoken by a person often reveal the true condition of the heart.

Chapter 13

Speech and the Tongue

Among all the ways the body expresses the inner life, none is more revealing than the words a person speaks because words give form to what is unseen. Speech is one of the primary ways the hidden life of the heart becomes visible. Thoughts may remain private for a time, and emotions may remain concealed, but words eventually reveal what resides within the inner person. Jesus explained this principle clearly when He said:

> *"For out of the abundance of the heart the mouth speaks." (Luke 6:45)*

According to this teaching, the mouth does not create what it says. Instead, it releases what already exists within the heart. Words become the outward expression of the inner life.

If the heart is filled with truth, encouragement, and devotion to God, those qualities will eventually appear in speech. If the heart is filled with anger, bitterness, or deception, those attitudes will also find expression through words. The tongue, therefore, serves as a bridge between the inner person and the outward world. Because of this, Scripture places great emphasis on the power of speech.

The book of James describes the tongue as a small part of the body with enormous influence. Just as a small rudder guides a large ship, the tongue has the ability to direct the course of human life. Words can encourage, guide, and strengthen others. They can also wound, discourage, and destroy.

Words of Exposure

The tongue reveals the condition of the heart. This connection between the heart and speech appears throughout Scripture. Words that bring life often flow from a heart that is aligned with God. Words that bring destruction often reveal a heart that is troubled or divided. For this reason, believers are encouraged to pay careful attention to their speech.

The goal is not merely to control words through self-discipline alone but to transform the source from which they come. This involves cultivating a heart that produces words consistent with the character of Christ. When the hidden man of the heart is aligned with God, the tongue begins to reflect that alignment. Instead of speaking words that produce division or harm, the believer learns to speak words that bring life. Encouragement replaces criticism. Truth replaces deception. Blessing replaces cursing.

It is possible, however, for a person to speak words that appear spiritual while the heart remains distant from God. Scripture warns against this kind of expression, often described as empty or hypocritical worship. A person may say that they love God, offer prayers, or speak words of praise, yet those expressions may not reflect a genuine inward relationship.

Jesus addressed this directly when He spoke to the Pharisees and scribes, saying, "These people honor me with their lips, but their heart is far from me" (Matthew 15:8). He went on to explain that worship offered in this way is in vain because it is disconnected from true devotion.

This kind of speech is often referred to as "lip service." It occurs when outward words are not supported by inward alignment. In such cases, faith becomes a performance rather than a relationship. Words are spoken, but they do not carry the weight of genuine belief.

For this reason, the goal is to live in such a way that the words spoken are consistent with what the heart truly believes. When the hidden man of the heart is aligned with God, speech becomes authentic. Words no longer attempt to create an appearance of devotion. They reveal a life that is genuinely devoted.

This transformation does not occur simply by deciding to speak differently. It begins with the condition of the heart. When the heart is renewed and the soul is unified under the leadership of the spirit, speech naturally begins to change. The believer becomes more aware of the power, or spiritual weight, carried by words.

Words of Power

Words can strengthen faith or weaken it. They can build trust or destroy relationships. They can reveal the truth of God or distort it. Because of this, the mouth becomes an important instrument in the life of faith.

Scripture connects speech directly with belief. As we saw earlier, the apostle Paul wrote that belief takes place in the heart and confession is made with the mouth. When the heart believes the truth of God's Word, the mouth expresses that belief.

The tongue becomes a tool through which faith is declared.

Confession of faith is not merely positive thinking or motivational language. It is the outward expression of conviction that has taken root within the heart. In this way, speech participates in the process of spiritual life. The heart believes, the soul agrees, and the mouth declares, bringing inward conviction into outward expression. This pattern reflects the design God placed within human nature.

Scripture also describes a remarkable transformation that occurred in the early church after the coming of the Holy Spirit. When believers were filled with the Spirit, their speech became empowered in new ways. They spoke with boldness, proclaimed the message of Christ, and supernaturally spoke in foreign languages, using their words to strengthen the community of faith and spread the gospel.

The same principle continues to apply to believers today. When the Spirit of God influences the heart, the words spoken by the believer begin to reflect divine truth and encouragement rather than personal opinion. Speech becomes an instrument through which God's purposes are expressed.

Yet the tongue must still be guarded carefully. Because speech carries such influence, careless words can cause harm even when the intention was not malicious. This is why Scripture encourages believers to think before speaking and to allow wisdom to guide their words.

A disciplined tongue reflects a disciplined inner life. When the hidden man of the heart is at peace with God, speech becomes more measured and thoughtful. The believer learns to speak in ways that reflect patience, kindness, and truth.

Through this transformation, the tongue becomes an instrument of life rather than an instrument of destruction. However, speech is not the only way the body reveals the inner life. Words are powerful, yet they are only one part of the outward expression of faith. Actions, choices, and daily conduct also reveal whether the spirit and soul are aligned with God.

If the tongue is capable of revealing what is within the heart, it is also capable of carrying what comes from God. This raises an important question: *What is the nature of the words that the believer is called to speak?*

To understand the responsibility of speech, we must first understand the nature of the Word itself.

The Purified Word and the Human Vessel

The words that proceed from God stand in complete contrast to the words of man. Scripture declares, "The words of the Lord are pure words: as silver tried in a furnace of earth, purified seven times" (Psalm 12:6). This image is not poetic exaggeration but a revelation of process. Silver is not found in isolation. It is extracted from ore, a substance filled with multiple elements, many of which must be burned away through intense heat before the silver can be revealed in its purity. In the same way, the Word of God comes forth through the "furnace of the earth," which is the human condition, yet remains untouched by corruption because it is purified by the Spirit of God.

This understanding addresses a question that has challenged many: How can an infallible Word come through fallible vessels? The answer is not found in human perfection but in divine process. The apostle Peter explains that "holy men of God spoke as they were moved by the Holy Spirit" (2 Peter 1:21). The vessel may be human, but the source is divine.

The refining work of the Spirit ensures that what proceeds from God retains its purity, even as it passes through human lips, minds, and hands. In other words, the Spirit preserves the integrity of what is spoken.

Criticism of Scripture often arises from misunderstanding this process. Some claim that the Bible is merely a human construct, shaped by culture or power, and therefore unreliable. Historical distortions such as the "Slave Bible," in which portions of Scripture were intentionally removed to control enslaved Africans in America, demonstrate that manipulation of the text has occurred. Yet such actions do not diminish the purity of God's Word. Instead, they reveal humanity's attempt to alter what cannot be corrupted at its source. The integrity of Scripture rests not in man's handling of it, but in God's authorship of it.

Furthermore, Scripture explicitly warns against adding to or subtracting from God's word, emphasizing its completeness and authority. Key warnings are found in Deuteronomy 4:2, 12:32; Proverbs 30:6; and Revelation 22:18-19, which mention severe consequences, such as incurring the plagues described in Revelation.

The prophets of the Old Testament and the teachings of Jesus both caution against false prophecy and the misuse of God's Word (Jeremiah 23; Matthew 7:15). The presence of misuse does not invalidate the Word; it underscores the need to understand it correctly.

The Furnace, the Fire, and the Word

To understand Psalm 12:6 more deeply, one must consider the full picture. The silver represents the Word of God. The furnace represents humanity, the earthly vessel through which the Word is expressed. The fire represents the Holy Spirit, who refines, purifies, and preserves the integrity of what God speaks. The reference to "seven times" signifies divine completeness and perfection. The Word is not partially purified. It is wholly refined, entirely trustworthy, and eternally true.

This process reveals that God does not bypass humanity; He works through it. He chooses vessels, prepares them, and refines them before entrusting them with His Word. The refining is often intense. It involves testing, correction, and surrender. Those who carry the Word are not selected based on worldly qualifications such as status, intellect, or influence. Scripture teaches that "God chose the foolish things of the world to shame the wise" (1 Corinthians 1:27), and that salvation itself comes "by grace...through faith...not by works" (Ephesians 2:8–9). The qualification is not human ability but divine calling and transformation.

This truth reshapes how we understand both Scripture and the act of speaking on behalf of God. The emphasis is not on the perfection of the messenger but on the faithfulness of the message. The vessel is refined so that the Word can pass through without distortion. In this way, fallibility is not a limitation but the very context in which God demonstrates His power.

The Mouth as an Instrument of Prophecy

The tongue, though small, carries immense spiritual significance. James writes that it has the power to bless and to curse, to build and to destroy (James 3:5–10). Within the life of the believer, the mouth becomes more than a means of communication. It becomes an instrument through which the Word of God is released into the earth. This is the essence of prophecy: not merely predicting future events, but declaring the truth, will, and promises of God under the guidance of the Holy Spirit.

Prophecy does not originate in human reasoning or personal interpretation. As Scripture makes clear, "no prophecy of the scripture is of any private interpretation" (2 Peter 1:20). The believer does not create the message but receives it. The responsibility is to speak what God has revealed, with accuracy, humility, and alignment with His Word. In this way, the mouth becomes a conduit through which heaven speaks into earthly situations.

This also explains why the enemy seeks to corrupt speech, as it carries influence. If the tongue can carry truth, it can also carry deception. If it can release life, it can also release destruction. The discipline of speech, therefore, is not optional in the spiritual life. It is essential. The believer must learn to align words with the purity of God's Word, allowing the Spirit to govern what is spoken.

Fallible Vessels, Infallible Word

The tension between human weakness and divine truth is not a flaw in God's design. It is part of His strategy. God deliberately chooses vessels that cannot take credit for the message they carry. This ensures that the glory remains with Him. The apostle Paul alludes to this principle when he describes believers as "earthen vessels" carrying a divine treasure (2 Corinthians 4:7).

This pattern continues today. Those who speak the Word of God are still being refined, still being shaped, and still being entrusted with a message that is greater than themselves. The same Spirit who inspired

Scripture continues to guide, correct, and empower those who declare it. The process has not changed. The Word remains pure. The Spirit remains active. The vessel remains human.

Understanding this removes both pride and doubt by placing confidence in the source, not the speaker. Pride is removed because the message does not originate with the speaker. Doubt is removed because the reliability of the Word does not depend on the perfection of the vessel. What matters is alignment with the Spirit and faithfulness to what God has spoken.

Speaking What Has Been Refined

The ultimate goal is not merely to understand the Word but to speak it with clarity and conviction. When the Word has been received, tested, and internalized, it begins to flow naturally from the life of the believer. Jesus taught that "out of the abundance of the heart the mouth speaks" (Matthew 12:34). What fills the inner life will inevitably shape outward expression.

This brings the discussion full circle. The Word of God is pure. It is refined, tested, and perfect. The believer, though human, is refined by the Spirit to carry that Word. The mouth then becomes the place where the invisible work of God becomes audible in the earth. In this way, speech is not merely communication. It is participation in the ongoing work of God.

When the believer understands this, the tongue is no longer used carelessly. It becomes a sacred instrument, aligned with truth, governed by the Spirit, and committed to declaring what God has said.

In the next chapter we will examine how the inner transformation of the heart and soul becomes visible through the way believers live – their actions, choices, and daily conduct.

Chapter 14

Conduct and Obedience

If the heart believes and the soul becomes aligned with the spirit, then the body must reveal that transformation through the way a person lives. Thus, true worship or devotion is not what is said with the mouth, but what is lived from the heart.

Spiritual life does not remain hidden within the inner person. It becomes visible through actions, decisions, relationships, and daily behavior. What a person does with their body reflects what the heart believes and what the soul has agreed to follow. For this reason, Scripture consistently connects faith with obedience because true faith produces action.

Faith is not merely an inward conviction. It expresses itself through the choices a person makes and the direction their life takes. When the spirit receives guidance from God and the soul aligns with that direction, the body becomes the instrument through which obedience is carried out. Hands perform acts of service. Feet carry the believer where God directs. The voice speaks truth and encouragement. Daily choices reflect devotion to God. In this way the physical life of a believer becomes a visible expression of the inward work of God.

The apostle Paul taught that believers should present their bodies to God as instruments of righteousness. This means that physical actions, such as what we do with our time, energy, and abilities, can be dedicated to the purposes of God. Rather than allowing the body to be guided by impulse or selfish desire, the believer learns to use the body as a tool for obedience.

This does not mean that spiritual life becomes rigid or mechanical. Instead, obedience becomes the natural outcome of a heart that trusts God and a soul that has been brought into alignment with His will. When the spirit leads and the soul cooperates, obedience becomes an expression of love.

Jesus Himself emphasized this connection when He taught that those who love Him will keep His commandments. Obedience is therefore not simply a matter of duty but a reflection of relationship. The believer obeys because the heart trusts the wisdom and goodness of God. Thus, obedience is love made visible.

This obedience also shapes the believer's relationships with others. The inward transformation produced by God's Spirit begins to affect how a person treats those around them. Patience replaces harshness. Kindness replaces indifference. Integrity replaces dishonesty. These outward behaviors are not simply moral improvements; they are signs that the inner life is being transformed.

Scripture often refers to this transformation as **bearing fruit** (John 15:1-5). Just as a healthy tree produces fruit that reflects its nature, a life aligned with God produces actions that reflect His character. Love, patience, gentleness, faithfulness, and self-control begin to appear in the daily conduct of the believer. These qualities do not emerge from human effort alone. They grow from the relationship between the believer and God.

As the spirit remains connected to the Spirit of God and the soul continues to align itself with truth, the body becomes the instrument through which this new life is expressed. Conduct therefore becomes a powerful testimony.

People may not see the hidden man of the heart, but they can observe the way a believer lives. They can see the patience displayed in difficult circumstances, the generosity shown toward others, and the courage demonstrated in moments of challenge. Through these actions the invisible work of God becomes visible in the world.

Yet obedience is not always easy. Situations arise where the path of obedience requires sacrifice, patience, or courage. In such moments the believer must rely again on the inner alignment that has been established between the spirit and the soul.

The spirit remembers the truth of God. The soul chooses to trust that truth. The body carries out the resulting action. In this way, obedience becomes the outward expression of faith. The believer learns to live not simply according to external pressures or circumstances but according to the inner guidance received from God. This is the restoration of the order that was disrupted.

This way of living transforms everyday life. Ordinary activities, such as work, conversation, service, and relationships, become opportunities to reflect the character of Christ. The believer's life gradually becomes a visible demonstration of what it means to live under the leadership of God. However, this transformation reaches its fullest expression when the entire person (spirit, soul, and body) begins to function together in harmony.

When the heart believes, the soul aligns, and the body obeys, the believer begins to live from the inside out consistently rather than occasionally.

Carrying the Gospel of Peace

In Paul's description of the armor of God, believers are instructed to have their feet fitted with the preparation of the gospel of peace. The imagery would have been familiar to Paul's readers. Roman soldiers wore specially designed footwear that allowed them to travel long distances and maintain stability in difficult terrain. Their ability to move quickly and stand firmly depended in large part on the shoes they wore.

Paul uses this image to describe the readiness believers should possess in carrying the message of the gospel. The good news of Christ brings peace between humanity and God, and those who receive that message are called to carry it into the world. Spiritual life does not remain confined to inward reflection. It moves outward through the actions and testimony of those who have experienced reconciliation with God.

This sense of readiness appears throughout the teachings of Jesus and the early church. After His resurrection, Jesus instructed His followers to go into all the world and proclaim the gospel to every creature. The message of salvation was never intended to remain hidden within a small circle of believers. Instead, it was meant to travel from person to person, crossing cultural boundaries and reaching every generation.

The gospel is called the message of peace because it announces the restoration of a broken relationship. Through Christ, the separation between humanity and God has been addressed, and reconciliation has become possible. When believers share this message, they carry with them the announcement that forgiveness, renewal, and new life are available to all who believe. For this reason, preparation becomes an essential part of the believer's life. Scripture encourages followers of Christ to study and understand the Word of God so they may communicate it faithfully. Readiness to speak about the hope of salvation requires both knowledge of the message and confidence in the One who sent it.

The movement described by Paul is not merely geographical; it is also relational. Believers bring the gospel into homes, workplaces, communities, and conversations where people are searching for meaning and hope. Every act of obedience, every word of encouragement, and every opportunity to speak about Christ becomes a step taken in the shoes of the gospel of peace. This demonstrates love for God in tangible form.

When believers live with this readiness, their lives become instruments through which the message of reconciliation continues to travel. The gospel moves forward through those who are willing to carry it, and the peace it announces reaches hearts that might otherwise remain untouched.

The Shield That Protects the Believer

Among the pieces of armor Paul describes, the shield occupies a particularly important place. Roman soldiers carried large shields that could protect nearly the entire body. When held firmly, the shield guarded the soldier from arrows, spears, and other projectiles launched from a distance. Paul draws on this familiar image to describe the role faith plays in the believer's life.

Faith functions as a protective barrier against the influences that seek to disturb the soul. Scripture speaks of "fiery darts" sent by the enemy, an image suggesting sudden thoughts, fears, accusations, or temptations that attempt to penetrate the mind. These attacks often arrive unexpectedly and may appear convincing at first glance. The shield of faith enables the believer to intercept those influences before they take root within the heart.

One of the remarkable aspects of faith is that people rely upon it continually, even when they do not recognize its presence. Every day individuals trust countless things they cannot see directly. They trust that a bridge will hold their weight, that a physician's advice is reliable, or that the rising sun will bring another day. Faith, in its most basic sense, involves trusting what has proven reliable even when the outcome cannot yet be seen.

In the spiritual life, faith rests upon the character and promises of God. Scripture explains that faith grows through hearing the Word of God. As believers become familiar with God's promises and His faithfulness throughout history, their confidence in Him begins to deepen. Faith is therefore not blind optimism but trust formed through relationship and understanding.

Because faith rests on God's character, it engages the entire person. The ears listen to the promises of God in Scripture. The eyes learn to recognize God's guidance in life. The heart begins to respond with gratitude and expectation. In this way faith gradually shapes how believers interpret their circumstances. Situations that once produced anxiety begin to be viewed through the lens of God's faithfulness.

When the shield of faith is raised, the believer no longer confronts life's challenges with uncertainty alone. Faith reminds the soul that God remains present and active even when circumstances appear difficult. Doubt, fear, and accusation may still approach, but they are prevented from penetrating the inner life because the shield stands between the believer and those influences.

For this reason, Paul encourages believers to take up the shield of faith above all. Faith does not eliminate the existence of difficulty, but it protects the heart and mind while those difficulties unfold. As believers continue to trust God's promises, their confidence grows, and the shield that once felt small becomes strong and steady.

Faith therefore serves not only as the beginning of the Christian life but also as its constant protection. It guards the believer in moments of uncertainty, strengthens perseverance during trials, and keeps the inner life anchored in the faithfulness of God.

The Word of God as the Sword

Among the pieces of spiritual armor described by the apostle Paul, only one is presented as an offensive weapon. The shield protects, the helmet guards the mind, and the breastplate covers the heart. The sword, however, is used to confront and defeat opposition. Paul identifies that weapon clearly when he writes about "the sword of the Spirit, which is the word of God." Through the Word, the believer speaks spiritual truth into situations that might otherwise be governed by fear, doubt or deception.

The power of this weapon does not lie merely in human speech. Scripture itself carries divine authority because it originates from God.

The Word reveals truth, exposes deception, and directs the believer toward the will of God. When the Word is understood and applied through faith, it becomes a living instrument through which the Spirit of God works in the life of the believer.

Learning to Trust the Word

Consider a simple illustration. Suppose you decide to bake a lemon pound cake using a boxed recipe that includes detailed instructions printed on the package. The directions are clear, and the method has been tested countless times by others. You follow the instructions carefully, expecting a beautiful cake to emerge from the oven. Instead, when the baking is finished, the cake has collapsed. It has sunk in the center and looks nothing like what you expected.

At that moment an important question arises. The instructions on the box have worked for many others, so where did the problem occur? You begin to examine your own process. Perhaps something was measured incorrectly, or perhaps the mixing time was not quite right. The failure does not necessarily mean the instructions were wrong. It may simply mean that the person following them has not yet mastered the process.

Rather than giving up, you try again. After several attempts you begin to understand the instructions more clearly. Over time you learn how to measure, mix, and bake with greater precision. Eventually the cake comes out perfectly. What once felt difficult becomes familiar, and the same instructions that once produced frustration now produce excellent results.

Faith Developed Through Practice

The Word of God functions in a similar way. Scripture contains promises and instructions that have been proven throughout generations of believers. When people begin to apply those promises in prayer or obedience, the results do not always appear when or how they expected. At times the believer may wonder whether the problem lies in the promise itself or in their own understanding of how to apply it. Moments like this can become opportunities for doubt. The soul may begin to question whether the Word truly works. Yet Scripture repeatedly encourages perseverance in faith. Just as skill develops through repeated practice, confidence in the Word of God grows as believers continue to apply it in daily life.

Jesus spoke about this kind of faith when He said, "Have faith in God... whoever says to this mountain, 'Be removed and cast into the sea,' and does not doubt in his heart but believes that what he says will happen, it will be done for him." The instruction is not an invitation to reckless speech but an encouragement to trust the authority of God's Word.

The Word That Pierces the Heart

Scripture also describes the Word of God in striking terms. The writer of Hebrews explains that the Word of God is living and powerful, sharper than any two-edged sword, capable of piercing even to the dividing of soul and spirit. It discerns the thoughts and intentions of the heart. This description reminds believers that the Word does more than provide instruction. It exposes what lies hidden within the human heart.

At times the Word confronts attitudes, motives, and desires that might otherwise remain unnoticed. In those moments the Spirit of God uses the Word as a surgical instrument, removing what does not belong and shaping the believer's character for God's purposes. The sword of the Spirit therefore works not only against spiritual opposition but also within the believer's own life.

When the Word Confronts the Heart

I experienced the penetrating power of God's Word in a very personal way during a season when pride had begun to take root in my heart. I owned a 1972 De Tomaso Pantera, a rare and powerful sports car that drew attention wherever it appeared. One afternoon, I was stopped at a traffic light near the corner of DeLowe Drive and Campbellton Road in Atlanta. As people gathered nearby, I began revving the engine loudly, enjoying the attention the car was attracting.

While I sat there filled with pride, the voice of God spoke quietly but unmistakably to my spirit. The message was direct: "Not only can I take the car from you, I can take you from the car." The moment those words came, everything changed. I drove directly home, parked the car, and sat quietly reflecting on what had just happened.

That experience revealed something important about the Word of God. When God speaks through His Word, there is no confusion about who is speaking. The message carries clarity and authority that cannot be ignored. The Word reaches beyond outward behavior and touches the deeper attitudes of the heart. In that moment, my pride had been exposed, and the Spirit of God used the Word to correct my life's direction.

The Living Power of the Word

The Word of God is therefore both corrective and life-giving at the same time. Scripture describes the Word as living and active, capable of bringing spiritual life where there was once spiritual death. Through the Word, the Holy Spirit awakens faith, renews understanding, and calls believers into deeper obedience.

For this reason, the Word of God functions as the sword of the Spirit in the believer's life. It confronts deception, exposes hidden motives, and directs the soul toward the purposes of God. When believers learn to trust and apply the Word faithfully, they discover that the sword of the Spirit remains one of the most powerful instruments God has given for spiritual growth and victory.

In the final chapter we will explore how this alignment of spirit, soul, and body produces a life that reflects God's design and allows the believer to walk in the fullness of their spiritual purpose.

Chapter 15

Living from the Inside Out

Human life was designed by God to function in harmony. Spirit, soul, and body were created to work together so that a person could live in relationship with God, understand themselves, and interact meaningfully with the world around them.

At this point, the pattern of spiritual life becomes clear. What begins in the heart, is shaped in the soul, and is expressed through the body was never meant to function separately, but as one unified life under the direction of God.

When these three dimensions operate according to God's design, life becomes balanced and purposeful. The spirit connects the person with God. The soul processes thoughts, emotions, and decisions. The body expresses those decisions through actions. However, when this order is disturbed, confusion often follows.

If the soul attempts to lead without guidance from the spirit, human reasoning and emotions begin to dominate life. Decisions become influenced primarily by circumstances, fears, and personal desires. Even when a person possesses knowledge or talent, something still feels incomplete.

Many people experience this sense of imbalance. They may develop their bodies through physical discipline or strengthen their minds through education and achievement, yet still feel that something is missing.

The reason for this emptiness is simple: the spirit was created to live in communion with God. Until that relationship is restored, life cannot fully function in harmony.

Scripture reminds us that "God is spirit" and that those who worship Him must worship in spirit and in truth (John 4:24). This means that the deepest relationship with God does not occur through the physical senses alone or through intellectual reasoning. It occurs within the spirit, the hidden man of the heart.

When a person believes in Christ, the spirit is renewed and reconnected with the source of life. This restoration becomes the foundation for spiritual growth. From that point forward, the believer begins to learn how to live from the inside out. The spirit receives guidance from the Holy Spirit. The soul gradually aligns with that guidance. The body expresses obedience through daily life.

As this alignment develops, the believer begins to experience a new sense of clarity and purpose. The spirit recognizes the voice of God. The soul becomes steadier as the mind is renewed. The body becomes an instrument for serving God and others. Life begins to reflect the design God intended.

This transformation does not mean that challenges disappear. Difficult situations continue to arise, and believers still encounter moments of uncertainty. Yet the foundation of life has changed.

Instead of being controlled by external circumstances, the believer learns to respond according to the truth received within the heart. Fear may attempt to influence the soul, but the spirit remembers God's promises. Doubt may arise in the mind, but the soul chooses to trust what God has spoken. Obedience may require courage, but the body acts according to the guidance received from within. In this way the believer gradually learns to live from the inside out.

This inward life also shapes the believer's relationship with others. As the spirit remains connected to God and the soul continues to align with His truth, the character of Christ begins to appear in daily conduct. Patience grows where frustration once dominated. Compassion replaces indifference. Faith replaces anxiety. The believer becomes a living testimony to the transforming power of God.

People may not see the hidden man of the heart, but they can observe the fruit produced in a life aligned with God. Words, actions, and relationships begin to reflect the inward work that God is performing. In this way the invisible work of the Spirit becomes visible through the lives of believers.

Standing Equipped for the Battle

Throughout Scripture the life of faith is often described as a journey, but the apostle Paul also describes it as a battle. The believer does not struggle against other human beings as enemies but against influences that seek to distort truth, weaken faith, and draw the soul away from God. For this reason, Paul uses the imagery of armor to describe the resources God has provided for those who follow Christ.

In the course of this book, the elements of that armor have appeared at different points because each one relates to a different dimension of the inner life. Truth forms the foundation of the renewed mind, establishing a stable understanding of God and His Word. The assurance of salvation guards the believer's thoughts against doubt and despair. Righteousness protects the heart, reminding the believer that through Christ a new standing with God has been established.

Faith then serves as a shield that protects the soul when accusations, fears, and temptations attempt to penetrate the mind. The gospel of peace directs the believer outward, calling those who have experienced reconciliation with God to carry that message to others. Finally, the Word of God functions as the sword of the Spirit, confronting deception and shaping the life of the believer through its penetrating truth.

Taken together, these images reveal something important about the Christian life. Spiritual strength does not arise from a single act of devotion or a moment of insight. It develops as the believer learns to live daily within the resources God has provided. Truth shapes understanding, faith protects the soul, righteousness guards the heart, and the Word of God directs the believer toward obedience.

When these elements work together, the believer becomes equipped to stand firmly even when circumstances are difficult. The armor of God is therefore not simply a collection of spiritual symbols, but a picture of a life formed by truth, protected by faith, and guided by the Spirit of God.

The goal of this preparation is not conflict for its own sake but faithfulness. God equips His people so that they may stand firm, remain faithful, and continue living in the light of His truth. As the inward life becomes aligned with God's design, the believer is able to face the challenges of the world with confidence, knowing that the resources necessary for the battle have already been provided.

A Life Aligned with God

The journey toward this kind of life is not completed in a single moment. It unfolds gradually as the believer continues to grow in understanding and obedience. The heart learns to trust God more deeply. The soul becomes more aligned with spiritual truth. The body becomes increasingly available for God's purposes. Ultimately, loving God with our *whole being* involves:

- **Heart / spirit → where love begins** (devotion, trust, faith)
- **Soul → where love is tested** (alignment, surrender, conflict)
- **Body → where love is expressed** (obedience, action, witness)

Over time the entire person begins to function in harmony with the Creator. Spirit, soul, and body, once divided by confusion and conflict, become unified under the leadership of God. This unity allows the believer to live with confidence, stability, and purpose.

The hidden man of the heart listens for the voice of God. The soul responds with trust and obedience. The body becomes the instrument through which God's work is expressed in the world. When this alignment takes place, life reflects the design God intended from the beginning. Believers learn to love God with all their heart, soul, and strength, not as separate parts competing for attention, but as a unified life devoted to Him. This is what it means to live from the inside out.

The Cleansed, Restored Life

The life described throughout this book is not made possible by human effort alone. It is rooted in the finished work of Jesus Christ. The same blood that was shed for the forgiveness of sin also cleanses the inner life, restoring what was broken and bringing the soul into alignment with God.

What was once stained has been made clean. What was once divided can now be made whole. Through Christ, the believer is not only forgiven but restored, able to live from the inside out with clarity, peace, and confidence in God.

This is the invitation that remains. To receive what has already been provided. To live from what has already been accomplished. To walk in a life that is no longer governed by the soul alone, but led by the spirit, renewed by truth, and sustained by the presence of God.

Praying for the Nations

As the life of faith matures, the focus of the believer gradually expands beyond personal spiritual growth. The transformation that begins within the heart and soul eventually turns outward toward the needs of others. One of the most powerful ways believers participate in God's work in the world is through prayer.

Scripture encourages believers to pray not only for personal concerns but also for the broader needs of society. The apostle Paul urged the church to offer prayers, intercessions, and thanksgiving for all people, including those who hold positions of authority. He explained that such prayers contribute to conditions in which people may live peaceful and godly lives. These instructions remind believers that prayer is not limited to private devotion but also serves as a means through which God's purposes unfold in the world.

Praying for leaders and nations requires a perspective shaped by the gospel. Human societies often experience conflict, injustice, and confusion, and it can be easy to respond with frustration or resentment. Scripture invites believers to approach these situations differently. Rather than reacting with hostility, followers of Christ are called to intercede for those who govern and influence communities, asking God to guide their decisions and bring wisdom where it is lacking.

This responsibility also reflects God's desire for humanity as a whole. Scripture declares that God desires all people to be saved and to come to the knowledge of truth. The mission of the church therefore extends far beyond its own gatherings. Believers participate in God's redemptive work whenever they pray for the well-being of cities, nations, and the people who inhabit them.

In a world where information about global events travels quickly, believers often become aware of crises and conflicts occurring far beyond their immediate surroundings. Rather than responding only with concern or debate, these moments can become invitations to prayer. News of political unrest, economic instability, or social division can prompt believers to ask God for wisdom, justice, and peace in those places.

When the church responds in this way, prayer becomes a form of spiritual service to the world. The believer who prays participates in God's work of guiding leaders, restraining injustice, and opening hearts to the message of salvation. Through prayer, the inward life that has been shaped by truth, faith, and righteousness begins to influence the broader human community.

In this way the journey described throughout this book reaches its outward expression. The heart learns to believe, the soul learns to follow the Spirit, and the body begins to live in obedience. From that foundation the believer becomes a participant in God's work among the nations, trusting that the same God who transforms individual lives also guides the course of human history.

A Life That Loves God Fully

From the beginning, this journey has been about understanding the inner life – what Scripture calls the heart, the soul, and the body – and how these work together in the life of a believer. What has been revealed is not merely structure, but purpose. Jesus declared, "You shall love the Lord your God with all your heart and with all your soul and with all your mind" (Matthew 22:37). This command is not abstract. It is deeply practical. It speaks to the totality of who we are.

To love God with the heart is to believe Him. It is in the hidden man of the heart that faith is formed, where the voice of God is heard, and where trust begins. Without this foundation, spiritual life cannot stand.

To love God with the soul is to bring the mind, emotions, and will into alignment with that faith. The soul must learn to agree with what the heart has received. This is where transformation takes place, where thoughts are renewed, emotions are steadied, and the will is surrendered to God.

To love God with the body is to express that inward reality through outward life. What is believed in the heart and formed in the soul must be lived through action. Obedience, worship, speech, and daily conduct become the visible evidence of an inward relationship with God.

When these are divided, conflict remains. The heart may believe while the soul resists. The soul may intend while the body fails to act. However, when they are brought into alignment, something powerful occurs. The believer begins to live from the inside out:

- The heart receives from God.
- The soul aligns with truth.
- The body expresses what has been formed within.

This is divine alignment, not perfection. It is a life continually being shaped, corrected, and restored by the Word of God and the work of the Spirit.

Through the blood of Jesus, the soul is cleansed, restored, and brought back into right relationship with God (Hebrews 10:19–22). What was once divided is made whole. What was once burdened is brought into peace. What was once distant is brought near.

So, the call remains, not simply to understand these truths, but to live them by believing with the heart, accepting the truth in the soul, and living it out through the body. This is the life Jesus described. This is the life made possible through Him. Most importantly, this is what it means to love God with your whole being.

Conclusion

Living Aligned with God

Throughout this book we have explored the inner design of human life as revealed in Scripture. The Bible teaches that human beings are more than physical creatures living in a material world. Each person is a spirit, possesses a soul, and lives in a body. Understanding this design has helped us uncover not merely a structure, but a way of life, one that reflects how God intended human beings to live in relationship with Him.

The spirit, the deepest dimension of the hidden man of the heart, was created to live in communion with God. It is the place where faith is born and where the voice of God can be heard. When a person believes the message of Christ, the spirit is renewed and restored to fellowship with its Creator. However, the work of transformation does not stop there.

The soul – the realm of thought, emotion, and decision – must learn to come into agreement with what the spirit has received from God. The mind must be renewed through the Word of God. The emotions must learn to rest in the promises of God rather than react to circumstances. The will must choose obedience over independence.

As the soul aligns with the spirit, inner conflict begins to diminish. The believer becomes more stable in thought, steadier in emotion, and more confident in the choices that reflect the wisdom of God. Eventually, this inward alignment becomes visible through the body. Words begin to change. Actions begin to reflect new priorities. Relationships begin to demonstrate patience, kindness, and faithfulness.

The life that once struggled with confusion begins to move with greater clarity and purpose. This is what it means to live from the inside out: the spirit listens to God, the soul agrees with the truth, and the body expresses that agreement through obedience. When these three dimensions work together, human life begins to reflect the design God intended from the beginning.

Yet this alignment does not occur automatically, and it is not achieved by effort alone, but by yielding to what God has already made possible through Christ. It requires a willingness to trust God, to renew the mind through His Word, and to allow the Spirit of God to shape the inner life day by day.

Spiritual growth is a journey. At times, the soul may struggle with doubt or fear. Circumstances may challenge faith. The pressures of life may attempt to pull attention away from the voice of God. However, the believer can always return to the same foundation: the hidden man of the heart where God speaks and where faith takes root. From that place, the soul can once again align itself with the truth of God's Word, and the body can once again walk in obedience.

As this process continues, the believer begins to experience a deeper sense of peace and confidence. Life becomes less driven by external pressures and more guided by the inward presence of God. This is the life Jesus described when He spoke of rivers of living water flowing from within. It is a life shaped by faith rather than fear, by obedience rather than uncertainty, and by trust rather than self-reliance.

When the heart believes, the soul aligns, and the body obeys, the believer learns to love God with the whole being: with heart, soul, and strength.

This is the life God desires for His people:

- A life not divided by inner conflict but unified under the leadership of His Spirit
- A life that reflects His wisdom, His peace, and His purpose
- A life that reveals, both inwardly and outwardly, the transforming power of God

This is the life that flows from a heart that believes, a soul that aligns, and a body that obeys. This is the life made possible through Christ and the life each believer is called to live.

www.ingramcontent.com/pod-product-compliance
Ingram Content Group UK Ltd.
Pitfield, Milton Keynes, MK11 3LW, UK
UKHW041829200726
13854UKWH00002BA/905

9 781733 640725